SO-BNE-389

Mountain Biking
South
Carolina

Nicole R. Blouin

FALCON®

HELENA, MONTANA

ＡFALCONGUIDE®

Falcon®Publishing is continually expanding its list of recreation guidebooks. All books include detailed descriptions, accurate maps, and all the information necessary for enjoyable trips. You can order extra copies of this book and get information and prices for other Falcon guidebooks by writing Falcon, P.O. Box 1718, Helena, MT 59624 or calling toll free 1-800-582-2665. Also, please ask for a free copy of our current catalog. Visit our web site at http://www.falconguide.com

© 1998 by Falcon® Publishing, Inc., Helena, Montana
Printed in the United States of America.

1 2 3 4 5 6 7 8 9 0 MG 03 02 01 00 99 98

Falcon and FalconGuide are registered trademarks of Falcon® Publishing, Inc.

All rights reserved, including the right to reproduce this book or parts thereof in any form, except for inclusion of brief quotations in a review.

All black-and-white photos by author unless otherwise noted.
Cover photo by Joshua Schaffer

Library of Congress Cataloging-in-Publication Data

Blouin, Nicole, 1966-
    Mountain biking South Carolina / by Nicole R. Blouin.
        p.   cm. — (A Falcon guide)
    ISBN 1-56044-684-6 (pbk.)
    1. All terrain cycling—South Carolina—Guidebooks. 2. Bicycle
trails—South Carolina—Guidebooks. 3. South Carolina—Guidebooks.
    I. Title. II. Series
    GV1045.5.S   IN PROCESS
    796.6'3' 09757--dc21   98-11814
                                                                    CIP

CAUTION

Outdoor recreational activities are by their very nature potentially hazardous. All participants in such activities must assume the responsibility for their own actions and safety. The information contained in this guidebook cannot replace sound judgment and good decision-making skills, which help reduce risk exposure, nor does the scope of this book allow for disclosure of all the potential hazards and risks involved in such activities.

Learn as much as possible about the outdoor recreational activities in which you participate, prepare for the unexpected, and be cautious. The reward will be a safer and more enjoyable experience.

♻ Text pages printed on recycled paper.

To Levi, my best friend for twelve years. Nothing in my life brought me such simple pleasure as being with you.

Levi relaxing after a ride.

Contents

Acknowledgments

As I traveled around the state, I was continually surprised at the willingness of both land managers and mountain bikers to help put this book together. The local bikers of South Carolina should be commended. They have worked hard, are extremely proud of their trails, and want to share their accomplishments.

Many people have contributed to making this project a reality. I'd like to send a big thank-you to Jim Schmid. I never could have done it without you, and that's the truth. We are lucky to have Jim in South Carolina as our state trails coordinator. Also, general information about the state's mountain bike trails came from Barry Loonan (Palmetto Cycling Coalition) and Tom Dalson (Palmetto Trails).

Thanks to my biking partners, photo models, and unofficial editors: Rob Edwards, Ashley Robinson, Lee McAbee, Erik Caldwell, Kirsten Slusar, Steve Bordonaro, and Brenda Blouin (Mom!). Sharon and Doug, thank you for the Thai food and the place to stay.

Also, special thanks to Jim Little with Anne Springs Close Greenway, Knight Cox with Clemson Experimental Forest, Paul Ellis with Greenville Parks and Recreation, Joseph Stevens with Santee Cooper Land Division, Kirk West with Charleston Department of Parks, Nancy Lindroth with Mecca Trails Association, Pat Metz with Pinckney National Wildlife Refuge, and Dean Harrigal with Donnelley Wildlife Management Area.

From the state parks, thanks to James Taylor at Paris Mountain, David Green at Santee, Ray Stevens at Hunting Island, and Robert Achenberg at Edisto. From the National Forest Service, thanks to Cheri Ramey (Long Cane District of Sumter), Alice Roads (Enoree District of Sumter), and Cheron Roads (Francis Marion). And from the state forests, thanks to Pete Spearman at Harbison.

Many cycle shops around the state are involved in trail building and maintenance. Of particular help were Tim Malson with Cycle Center in Columbia, Jeff and Craig with Sunshine Cycle in Clemson, Robert Baker with College Cycles in Rock Hill, and Grant Wallace with Great Escape in Spartanburg.

Local rider Bill Victor with Augusta Freewheelers deserves a lot of credit for all his help with the trails around McCormick. And thanks to the Clemson Cycling Club and the Greenville Spinners.

Several good rides came to my attention late. I'd like to thank the following people for putting together the information necessary to get these trails in the book at the last minute: Tim Bateman for Sand Hills Mountain Bike Trail, Rick Attaway for Lynches Woods Trail, Lee McAbee and Grant Wallace for Tour de Dump, and Don Brion from West Ashley Greenway.

My final acknowledgment goes to Falcon Publishing. Thank you for giving me this wonderful opportunity to ride and write about the great mountain bike trails in South Carolina.

Map Legend

Interstate		Campground	
U.S. Highway		Picnic Area	
State or Other Principal Road		Buildings	
Forest Road		Peak/Elevation	4,507 ft.
Interstate Highway		Bridge/Pass	
Paved Road		Gate	
Gravel Road		Parking Area	
Unimproved Road		Boardwalk/Pier	
Trail (singletrack)		Railroad Track	
Trailhead		Cliffs/Bluff	
Trail Marker		Power Line	
Waterway		Forest Boundary	
Intermittent Waterway		Map Orientation	N
Lake/Reservoir		Scale	0 0.5 1 MILES
Meadow/Swamp			

Statewide Locator Map

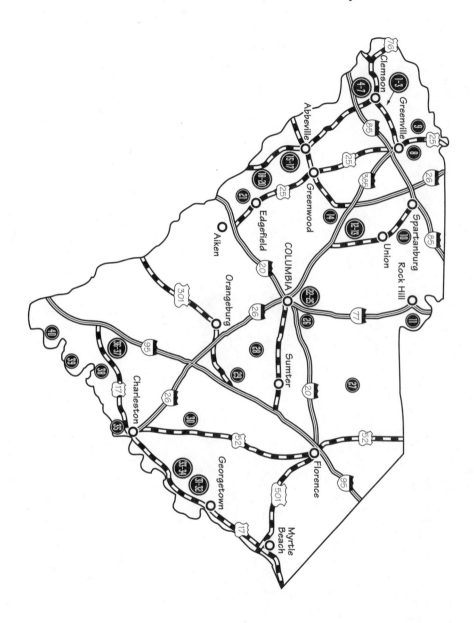

Introduction

Come discover some of the best mountain bike rides in the Palmetto State. South Carolina offers excellent trails from the foothills of the Blue Ridge Mountains to the sandy beaches along the Atlantic Ocean. Each region of the state is represented in this book, and I invite you to try the challenging and technical trails in the rolling hills of the Upstate, the fast singletrack of the Piedmont, and the relatively flat, scenic paths through the swampland or along the lakeshore of the Lowcountry.

South Carolina's miles of well-maintained singletrack, plus the state's outstanding scenery and weather, equal great mountain biking. One popular trail utilizes an old railroad logging tram, and another follows a public utility dike system along the edge of a large lake. Some of the best singletrack is within minutes of the capital city.

The rides in this book travel through South Carolina's public greenways, wildlife refuges, city and state parks, and state and national forests. There are easy trails for the novice rider and more adventurous roller-coaster runs for the expert.

What are you waiting for? Hop on your bike and begin adding up the miles on some of the best mountain biking trails in South Carolina.

TOPOGRAPHY, WEATHER, AND HAZARDS

South Carolina's topography ranges from the rolling mountains to the coastal plain. The state's northwestern corner, often called the Upstate, is my favorite because I love the mountains (I was lucky enough to live and work on the Chattooga River for ten years). The area lies in the foothills of the Blue Ridge Mountains, home to waterfalls, old-growth forests, and whitewater rivers, just to name a few of the attractions—Sassafras Mountain, elevation 3,560 feet, is the highest point in the state.

Unfortunately, there are few mountain bike trails in the heart of these beautiful mountains. The majority of the rides are concentrated in the rolling hills of Clemson's Experimental Forest, which is great riding; and Greenville and Spartanburg each have something worthwhile. But the Andrew-Pickens Ranger District of Sumter National Forest and the area around Lake Jocassee have yet to be developed for the most part because of the distance to a city.

The Lowcountry of South Carolina, a mix of ocean, barrier islands, salt marsh, forest, and farmland, offers a different type of challenge. Most mountain bikers will approach the Lowcountry with a degree of skepticism because there is no appreciable elevation change, but there is actually some fun singletrack along the coast. You'll ride through tunnels of massive live oaks dripping with Spanish moss; you'll ride right on the beach, passing sand dunes and sea oats; and you'll ride on raised dikes around impounded waters that were once used to cultivate rice and now service waterfowl and wading birds. Much of the beauty of the Lowcountry is protected from development; it has been designated as state parks, national forests, and wildlife management areas.

The Lowcountry also includes an area known as Santee-Cooper, where a hydroelectric project created two large freshwater lakes in the late 1930s: Lake Moultrie and Lake Marion. Located about 60 miles from the Atlantic Ocean, each offers unique biking opportunities.

The land between the mountains and the coast is called the Piedmont, but it actually includes at least two distinct regions. The Upper Piedmont, where much of riding is on the red clay soil of Sumter National Forest, runs from Columbia north to Greenville. This area includes an "inland coast," a string of dams and reservoirs built by the U.S. Army Corps of Engineers that have turned the western border of the state into almost one continuous lake. The capital city, Columbia, lies in an area of the Piedmont known as the Midlands. Columbia is in the middle of the state and is home to a lot of well-maintained singletrack because of the large population of enthusiastic mountain bikers. The Sandhills, east of Columbia, is a land of huge hills of sand deposited by an ancient sea. Two state forests—Manchester and Sand Hills—offer roller-coaster riding on hard-packed, sandy singletrack.

The weather in South Carolina allows mountain bikers to ride year-round. You will find long summers and mild winters. Winter temperatures generally average in the 40s and 50s inland and in the 60s along the coast. There are occasional snowfalls and some awfully cold rainy days in the western part of the state, but that's not typical weather. Summers are hot and humid, especially along the coast, with highs often in the 90s. Milder temperatures from 70 to 80 in the Upstate make summer rides tolerable.

As with many areas, spring and fall are the best times for riding if you want to avoid extremes. Pleasant temperatures along with wildflowers and fall foliage make these seasons comfortable and enjoyable.

Other things to consider: The summer is the worst period for mosquitoes, especially on barrier islands and in marshy areas. Gnats and ticks are also a problem. Keep your distance from alligators, which roam in many areas along the coast. Poisonous snakes can be found throughout the state, although they're rarely encountered by mountain bikers. Always think "hunters" when riding in national or state forests in the fall and winter. And be sure to contact the individual office where you are going to check on specific dates and regulations.

Average Temperatures

Highs/Lows in degrees Fahrenheit

	January	April	July	October
Upstate	51/31	73/48	88/68	72/49
Piedmont	56/33	77/50	92/70	76/50
Lowcountry	59/40	76/56	89/74	77/59

HOW TO USE THIS GUIDE

The book includes 40 rides, each with a ride number in front of the trail's name on the statewide locator map, in the table of contents, and on the maps. In addition to these rides, some of the ride descriptions list bonus rides and give a contact to help you find out about more miles to be biked in the area.

I've tried to include as many details as possible to help make your ride a success, but before you go, be sure to contact the land manager, local bike shop, or mountain bike club listed to get updated information. Addresses and phone numbers appear in the appendices.

The following headers are used for each ride to give specifics about what to expect from the trail.

Location: This describes the general area in the state where you'll find the ride, referenced to the nearest major cities or other landmarks.

Distance: This number provides the length of the ride in miles, as well as the configuration. A trail will be described as a loop (total miles), an out and back (total miles), or one way (mileage in one direction).

Tread: This description tells you what type of surface you'll be riding on, as well as a note about conditions.

Aerobic level: The physical challenge of the topography is explained here. Rides are rated easy, moderate, or strenuous. The aerobic exertion depends on the person, but the following gives you a guideline for understanding the level.

Easy: Relatively flat; elevation change is barely noticeable.

Moderate: Rolling hills; a handful of good climbs.

Strenuous: Longer and steeper climbs; some cyclists may have to walk short sections.

Technical difficulty: This scale quantifies the technical skill needed for a ride. Trails are rated on a scale of 1 to 3, with a + or - added for further delineation.

1: Basic riding skills needed. Mostly smooth with minor obstacles including roots, ruts, or rocks.

2: Some irregular tread. Tight turns, narrow trail, and a few rough spots.

3: Good technical singletrack. Some specialized skill needed to stay in the saddle on sidehills, log jumps, or whoop-dee-do's. Expect continuous sections of uneven, eroded trail, plus challenges on climbs or descents.

Land status: Most of the rides are on public land and this information is listed here. Land ownership occasionally changes, so be aware of trailhead bulletins or other posted signs indicating such.

Maps: The USGS 7.5 quadrangle is provided for every ride. Other maps that may be more useful can be obtained from land managers and bike shops, which are listed in the appendices.

Access: This information will assist you in finding the trailhead. If the ride is one way, directions for shuttling a second vehicle are also included.

Highlights: These paragraphs detail the qualities that make a ride unique. You'll find specifics on things you'll see along the way and a general description of natural surroundings.

The ride: Mileage readings, starting with 0.0 at the trailhead, will help you keep your bearings along the way. I recommend purchasing a cyclometer.

RIDING RIGHT: IMBA RULES OF THE TRAIL

As mountain bikers, it is our responsibility to know the trail and use common courtesy when riding. A few abusive riders can close a trail for everyone. The International Mountain Bike Association (IMBA) promotes the following guidelines. Check out this list, ride responsibly, and do your part to keep us from being excluded from trails in the future. The IMBA Rules of the Trail are as follows:

1. Ride on open trails only. Respect trail and road closures (ask if not sure), avoid possible trespass on private land, obtain permits and permission where required. Federal and state wilderness areas are closed to cycling. The way you ride will influence trail management decisions and policies.

2. Leave no trace. Be sensitive to the dirt beneath you. Even on open (legal) trails, avoid riding immediately after heavy rain or when the trail surface is soft and muddy. In some locations, muddy trails are unavoidable. Recognize different types of soils and trail construction; practice low-impact cycling. This also means staying on existing trails and not creating new ones. Be sure to pack out at least as much as you pack in.

3. Control your bicycle. Inattention for even a second can cause problems. Obey all bicycle speed regulations and recommendations.

4. Always yield trail. Give your fellow trail users plenty of notice when you approach. A friendly greeting (or bell) is considerate and works well; don't startle others. Show your respect when passing by slowing to a walking pace or even stopping, particularly when you meet horses. Anticipate other trail users around corners or in blind spots.

5. Never scare animals. All animals are startled by an unannounced approach, sudden movements, or loud noise. This can be dangerous for you, others, and the animals. Give animals extra room and time to adjust to you. When passing horses use special care and follow directions from the horseback riders (ask if uncertain). Running cattle and disturbing wildlife is a serious offense. Leave gates as you found them, or as marked.

6. Plan ahead. Know your equipment, your ability, and the area in which you are riding—and prepare accordingly. Be self-sufficient at all times, keep your equipment in good repair, and carry necessary supplies for changes in weather or other conditions. A well-executed trip is a satisfaction to you and not a burden or offense to others. Always wear a helmet.

GETTING INVOLVED

Mountain biking is catching on fast here in South Carolina. In January 1996, the South Carolina Mountain Bike Association, now the Palmetto Cycling

Coalition (PCC), was established to promote the sport throughout the state. The club constructs and maintains trails, deals with access issues, and publishes a newsletter.

PCC needs your help; they can help you find out who manages your favorite trail so you can volunteer close to home. Individuals and local clubs play a vital role in trail maintenance. Do something for our sport by putting something back into the trail.

In addition to being a part of an organization in South Carolina, consider joining the International Mountain Bike Association (IMBA). This nonprofit organization of off-road cyclists promotes environmentally sound and socially responsible mountain biking. Get involved or we might lose access to our mountain bike trails.

THE PALMETTO TRAIL

The construction of a mountaj < Ç-to-sea trail in the Palmetto State is well under way. When completed, the Palmetto Trail will stretch from the Lowcountry along the Atlantic coast to the foothills of the Blue Ridge Mountains at Oconee State Park. This 430-mile passageway will consist of new and existing trails through state parks, national forests, private lands, and historic sites. Different parts of the trail will be designated for hikers, horseback riders, and of course, mountain bikers.

The trail is being opened in sections (called passages). These are stretches of trail that can be hiked in about two to three days. Lake Moultrie, the first passage, opened in 1995. Passages are expected to be finished every few months until 2000, the proposed completion date of the project.

The Palmetto Trails Association, which promotes the development of the Palmetto Trail, as well as other state trails and greenways in South Carolina, publishes a general brochure on the trail that includes inserts on each passage as it opens. When this book went to press, four passages of the Palmetto Trail were in use. For general information, contact the Palmetto Trails Association (see Appendix A).

For more information on the Palmetto Trail, see the Future Trails section of this book. Following are detailed descriptions of the four open passages.

Swamp Fox Passage: This 42-mile passage travels through South Carolina's Lowcountry in Francis Marion National Forest, extending from U.S. Highway 17 in Awendaw, north of Charleston, to the Canal Recreation Area at Lake Moultrie on US 52. Swamp Fox is the easternmost passage of the Palmetto Trail. The first 13 miles of this trail are covered in Ride 33.

Lake Moultrie Passage: Mountain bikers can ride all 27 miles of this passage, which follows the northern shoreline of Lake Moultrie. The first link of this trail is covered in Ride 30.

High Hills Trail of the Santee Passage: This 14-mile passage, located in the Sandhills region at Manchester State Forest, connects Poinsett State Park and Mill Creek County Park. High Hills isn't covered in the book because it is primarily an equestrian trail, and most mountain bikers ride the

The Palmetto Trail

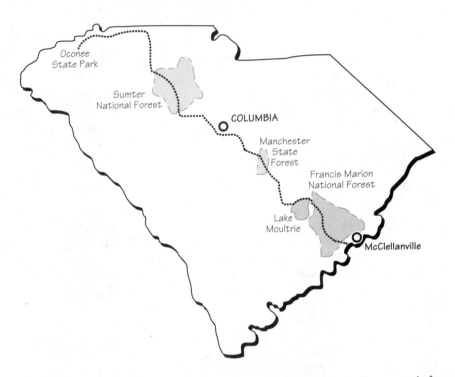

popular Killer Three Loop (Ride 28) when visiting the area. For more information, contact Manchester State Forest (see Appendix A).

Buncombe Trail of the Sumter Passage: Mountain bikers are welcome on 9 of 14 miles of the completed portion of the Sumter Passage, which runs along the southern border of Sumter National Forest northwest of Columbia. This portion of the trail is covered in Ride 13.

FUTURE TRAILS

The future of mountain biking in South Carolina looks bright. Trails are continually being developed throughout the state. The changes are happening so fast that the manuscript for this book was already in need of updates a month or so after it reached the publisher. For this reason, the following section of the book will try to predict the future in order to keep you up-to-date.

Sometimes it's two steps forward and one step back. A good example is the trail at Sand Hills State Forest, one of the state's newest singletrack loops. Local riders have worked hard to put this trail together and are excited about its place in this guide (see Ride 27). But during the year I worked on this book, two different sections of their trail were clearcut and had to be rerouted. If you had shown up to ride during that time, the trail wouldn't have been as you expected.

In many areas of the state, parking lots are being built to accommodate the growing numbers of mountain bikers, and trails rerouted to fix problems with erosion and avoid conflicts with horse traffic. Jim Schmid, our state trails coordinator, encourages folks to check out the government web site to find out about trail closures, new trails, and trail modifications (see Appendix A).

Some of the following rides will be ready to use before the publication of this book; others should be ready within a year, and unfortunately, a few will never be completed. John Kirby with the Palmetto Cycling Coalition hopes that mountain bikers will consider joining this statewide organization. The stronger and more organized we are as a group, the better our chances of improving and protecting access to existing trails, and at the same time ensuring the construction of new trails.

But for now, read on to the learn about the exciting possibilities for the future of mountain biking in the Palmetto State.

In the Upstate

Greenville

The Greenville Parks and Recreation department is planning a trail on some city-owned land east of Interstate 85 near Mauldin Road. By the spring of 1999, mountain bikers in the area will finally have a good place to ride—great news for the Greenville riders who have been frustrated with Paris Mountain State Park and who have lost their trails on Umbro's land to development. This trail will be built specifically for mountain bikers, but the distance is still uncertain, as are parking and access. If you know the area, the land is near the rifle range, on the other side of the Reedy River. Access to this tract is through a county neighborhood. For more information on this project's progress, contact Greenville Parks and Recreation (see Appendix A).

Jocassee Gorge

The Department of Natural Resources project to acquire 32,000 acres of land in Jocassee Gorge is finally complete. A gift of $10 million from a private foundation came with the stipulation that a management plan be in place by May 1998; the plan has been approved and mentions mountain bikers specifically. This sought-after tract is north and east of Lake Jocassee, with some sections close to the Cherokee Foothills Scenic Highway (South Carolina 11). There is great potential for recreational use, including mountain biking, and there is talk of the state parks along SC 11 becoming gateways to the gorge, with state park trails running into Jocassee. Currently, mountain bikers can ride legally on all established logging roads, and a mountain biking trail is under consideration. For more information about the management of Jocassee Gorge, contact the South Carolina Department of Natural Resources (see Appendix A).

Clemson Experimental Forest

If you've been to the Upstate, you know most of the best singletrack is in the Clemson Experimental Forest—Issaqueena Lake and Fants Grove. During 1997, the forestry department at Clemson University made several improvements, including new trail signs and large parking lots at both areas. But the best news is yet to come.

In the spring of 1998, a public meeting was held to discuss the possibility of a management plan for the trails at the experimental forest. A new mountain bike group called the Greater Clemson Mountain Bikers Club was formed; the sole purpose of this club is to support the university's adaptive management plan. This community-based organization will be involved in future regulation and maintenance of Issaqueena Lake and Fants Grove. Clemson's Experimental Forest may be the first piece of public land in South Carolina to have a plan for managing trails.

Also, the forestry department is working to obtain Global Positioning System coordinates to all the trails and create a map for its users. Rough drafts are posted at trailhead bulletin boards. For availability of this map and for information concerning the implementation of the management plan, contact Clemson Experimental Forest or the Greater Clemson Mountain Bikers Club (see Appendix A).

Palmetto Trail

The Palmetto Trail is finally making its way to the Upstate. A passage is in the works near where Interstate 26 crosses the border into North Carolina. The 13-mile trail begins at the Foothills Equestrian Nature Center, crosses several private holdings, passes the town of Landrum, and heads into the Landrum Watershed. However, there is a catch! The representative of Palmetto Trails I spoke with is not sure if this passage will allow mountain bikers; but if it does, it will be a superb ride. For more information about this trail, contact the Palmetto Trails Association (see Appendix A).

In the Piedmont

Baker Creek State Park

Members of the Augusta Freewheelers are building an 8-mile trail of singletrack from scratch at Baker Creek State Park, which is near the Long Cane District of Sumter National Forest. This trail is one of the first in South Carolina to be built and maintained by cyclists. It is a great addition to the booming mountain bike mecca around McCormick.

Baker Creek consists of the rolling country bordering Lake Thurmond. It offers recreators the opportunity to camp near the trailhead. To reach the state park, head west out of McCormick on U.S. Highway 378 for 3.7 miles and turn right at the sign for Baker Creek. Travel another mile or so and turn left into the park. The trailhead is located at the back of the park, near the pavilion.

As this book went to print, the trail was about 50 percent completed; to receive full funding, the project must be finished by October 1998. For more information, contact Baker Creek State Park or the Augusta Freewheelers (see appendices A and C).

Mecca Trails Association

The Mecca Trails Association (MTA) includes several interested groups in a three-county area who want to improve and promote trails in and around the Long Cane Ranger District of Sumter National Forest. MTA recently received funding for a part-time coordinator and will soon have its own address. Expect big things to happen around McCormick. Contact the McCormick Chamber of Commerce for more information (see Appendix A).

Santee State Park

The folks at Santee State Park are constructing a new trail off the Lakeshore Trail (see Ride 29). The trail is located in the triangle of land between State Park Road, Cleveland Road, and the lakeshore. Plans suggest a trail closer to the lake, as well as a large loop off the existing out and back. For more information, contact Santee State Park (see the appendix).

Jackson Passage

Passages of the Palmetto Trail (the state's mountains-to-sea trail) will continue to open over the next few years. A section is planned through Fort Jackson, one of the nation's largest U.S. Army training grounds, and could be open by late fall of 1998.

This huge tract of land on the eastern border of Columbia is easily larger than the city itself. The developed area of Fort Jackson is relatively small, leaving woodlands, sandhills, and wetlands preserved from urban sprawl. Road bikers have been riding here for years, and now mountain bikers will be able to enjoy 17 miles of mostly singletrack through a forest of tall long-leaf pines and some sections of hardwoods.

This ride will begin just inside Fort Jackson's main gate and wind through the woods away from the training areas. The trail will close after dark. At this point, the trail builders are waiting for official approval. Most of the trail is already mapped and flagged. For information about the Jackson Passage, contact the Palmetto Trails (see Appendix A).

Manchester State Forest

Things are happening at Manchester State Forest. A new parking lot for the Killer Three Loop (Ride 28) is being built on the left side of Park Road (State Route 63) a few tenths of a mile before River Road. Mountain bikers can go out the front of the parking lot to access their trail, while the equestrians can head out the back. Some rerouting to the loop is planned to further separate the bikes and the horses.

Poinsett State Park, adjacent to Manchester, is in the process of obtaining 7 miles of abandoned railroad land from Norfolk Southern for the construction of a rail-trail. A bridge connecting the back side of the state park to the swamp is already complete. The entire project will be slow and costly, but will eventually offer bikers a scenic ride along the Wateree River in addition to the area's mountain bike loop.

For information about the modifications to the Killer Three Loop, contact Manchester State Forest or Buddy's Schwinn Cycling and Fitness. To learn more about the rail-trail, contact Poinsett State Park (see appendices A and B).

In the Lowcountry

Swamp Fox Passage

While the Lowcountry may not be known for its mountain biking, it should be known that the final section of the easternmost passage of the Palmetto Trail was finished early in 1998 and now extends inland 42 miles, from the coastal town of Awendaw along U.S. Highway 17 to the eastern shore of Lake Moultrie. By combining the Swamp Fox Trail (Ride 33) with the next passage, Lake Moultrie (Ride 30), you get 68 miles of uninterrupted riding through Lowcountry swampland and pine forest, and around the shoreline of Lake Moultrie. See Ride 33 for information about the first 13 miles of the Swamp Fox Passage. Here you will find directions to the eastern trailhead in Awendaw. For directions to the western trailhead at the Canal Recreation Area on Lake Moultrie, see Ride 30.

The Witherbee Ranger Station acts as a middle trailhead if you want to shorten the distance of this passage. To reach the ranger station from Awendaw on U.S. Highway 17, take Steed Creek Road (State Route 133) to its intersection with South Carolina 41. Cross SC 41 onto SR 402. Travel about 3 miles and turn right on Copperhead Road (SR 125). You'll reach a T intersection after 2 miles. Turn right and locate the ranger station within 0.5 mile on the right.

The final stretch of the Swamp Fox Passage to be completed is called the Wadboo section. Trail builders, primarily young people who are Americorp volunteers, had to find a way to get trail users across Wadboo Swamp. In addition to many small bridges, they also built an unusual, 120-foot bridge that they had to actually wrap around trees in places; you will probably have to walk your bike through this section. For more information about this lengthy mountain bike ride, contact Palmetto Trails, as well as the Witherbee Ranger District of Francis Marion National Forest (see Appendix A).

The Upstate

There is no doubt that the northwestern corner of South Carolina includes some of the most scenic parts of the state. Here, the southern end of the Blue Ridge Mountains dips into South Carolina. This is a land of mountain ridges, rushing streams, sheer rock cliffs, and breathtaking waterfalls.

Much of this pristine beauty is protected in the Andrew-Pickens Ranger District of Sumter National Forest. Here, you'll find the Chattooga River, officially designated a Wild and Scenic River by Congress. This waterway forms part of the western border of the state and provides class I through class V rapids. A whitewater rafting trip is a great way to enjoy the wildness of the area and take a break from the saddle of your bike. Contact Wildwater, Ltd. for information (see Appendix A). They offer trips for all levels of ability.

Visit Lower Whitewater Falls to see the most impressive waterfall in the state. The Whitewater River drops 400 feet before flowing into Lake Jocassee. Another popular destination is Raven Cliff Falls near Caesars Head. Pick up a brochure on the waterfalls in Oconee, Pickens, and Greenville counties from the ranger station on U.S. Highway 28 north of Walhalla.

Elevations in the Upstate reach over 3,000 feet. Sassafras Mountain (3,554 feet) stands the tallest. Then the topography gently falls away to the southeast into the rolling foothills of the Piedmont.

When visiting the Upstate, consider staying at one of several state parks along the Cherokee Foothills Scenic Highway (South Carolina 11). Or just take a drive on this two-lane road as it winds along the base of the mountains past Devil's Fork, Keowee-Toxaway, Table Rock, and Caesars Head. Enjoy primitive camping or upscale accommodations at these state parks.

Spring is incredible in the Upstate and a great time to ride. I always look forward to the burst of color from the thickets of laurel in May, followed by the rhododendron blooms in early June. Also, you'll pass by many orchards throughout the Upstate. Peach and apple trees produce a sweet fragrance along with their attractive blossoms.

On many of my rides in the Upstate, I saw white-tailed deer and wild turkeys. Raccoons, squirrels, rabbits, foxes, and beavers live here as well. While seldom seen, black bears are making a remarkable recovery in the area.

The trees that shade your rides in this part of the state include oak, hickory, maple, poplar, and pine. My favorite part of the upland forest is the towering hemlock groves. The foliage of varied hardwoods draws visitors to the Upstate in the fall. You can see brilliant displays of orange, yellow, and red toward the end of September.

You'll find commercial development along Interstate 85 and the Upstate's largest city—Greenville. This is one of the fastest growing regions in the nation because businesses from around the world have put down roots here. Greenville is a good base for a visit to the Upstate if you enjoy the amenities that come with a city. Be sure to check out the downtown plaza known as the Common, as well as Reedy River Falls Historical Park—a riverside greenway, also located downtown—which provides picnicking, landscaped gardens, and bike paths.

Because many of the rides in the Upstate are located in Clemson's Experimental Forest, a visit to the university town of Clemson is in order. (Go Tigers!) To get the best milkshake around, go to Uniquely Clemson in Newman Hall, where the university sells its famous dairy products.

For travel information concerning the Upstate, contact the Discover UpCountry Carolina Association (see Appendix A). Welcome centers are located, as you enter the state, from Georgia on Interstate 85, and from North Carolina on I-26.

Clemson Experimental Forest

Clemson University owns 17,500 acres of southern upland forest called the Clemson Experimental Forest. Two areas, Issaqueena Lake and Fants Grove, offer miles of mountain biking on singletrack, old logging roads, and maintained gravel roads.

The government had the foresight to buy the land in the 1930s when the forest was rapidly disappearing. Red hills, river bottoms, and cow pastures covered the area, and about 75 percent of the topsoil was gone. But during the 1940s, Clemson University reclaimed the land for the government, and in 1954 it was deeded to the school to be preserved as an outdoor laboratory for teaching forest management.

Issaqueena, the forest north of Clemson, is made up of approximately 8,000 acres. It was established as a recreation area as early as the 1930s, before the lake was created. Then, the dam on Six Mile Creek formed Issaqueena Lake, the only large lake in the area at the time. Issaqueena has several small recreation areas with parking lots and picnic tables. Compared with Fants Grove, the trails at Issaqueena tend to be flatter and faster.

Fants Grove, the forest south of Clemson, encompasses approximately 9,000 acres and remains fairly primitive. At Fants Grove, you will find more miles, steeper hills, and harder terrain. While the trails at both areas have some erosion problems and will be muddy after a rain, Fants is worse because of more horse traffic. (Note: Please yield to horses when riding in both areas.)

While the primary goal of the forest is academic, the Clemson Experimental Forest is open to the public for outdoor recreation. You will encounter hikers, hunters, horseback riders, and of course, fellow mountain bikers. The Department of Forest Resources plans to develop more trails in both areas. Contact the Clemson Experimental Forest or the Clemson Cycling Club to find out what you can do to help maintain this resource (see appendices A and C).

Issaqueena Lake Trail

Location:	4 miles north of Clemson University in the Indian Springs Recreation Area at Issaqueena Lake.
Distance:	7.8 miles out and back.
Tread:	Singletrack with 0.6 mile on old roadbed.
Aerobic level:	Moderate; one significant climb.
Technical difficulty:	3-; tight switchbacks, tree roots, several creek crossings, and drop-offs to the lake. The most technical move on the ride is out along the lake—a challenging, rideable rock slab.
Land status:	Clemson University.
Maps:	USGS Clemson; an inexpensive map from Sunshine Cycle in Clemson.
Access:	From the junction of U.S. Highway 123 and South Carolina 133 in Clemson, take SC 133 north toward Six Mile. Travel 3.6 miles and turn left onto Old Six Mile Highway, just past Maw's Grocery. Go 0.1 mile and turn right onto Issaqueena Main Road. The parking lot for Indian Springs Recreation Area is 0.5 mile on the left. (From November 1 to March 15, Issaqueena Main Road is closed. Continue 0.5 mile past Issaqueena Main Road and park on the right at the lot before Issaqueena Dam Road. Ride back to Issaqueena Main Road and down to Indian Springs Recreation Area.)

HIGHLIGHTS

This trail is the most popular ride at Issaqueena Lake, and for good reason. The extremely fast singletrack combined with the scenic miles along the lake make an excellent ride. Before you begin this loop, spread out a picnic on one of the tables at the recreation area and take some time to appreciate this rehabilitated forest.

While relatively flat, this singletrack requires a moderate degree of technical skill, which is why this stretch is used by the Clemson Cycling Club as part of a race course. Slow down when you reach the lake to wind in and out of the lakeside coves. Early morning fog often hangs above the water—a spectacular scene in autumn.

Issaqueena Lake Trail • Dalton Road Ride • Figure Eight at Holly Springs

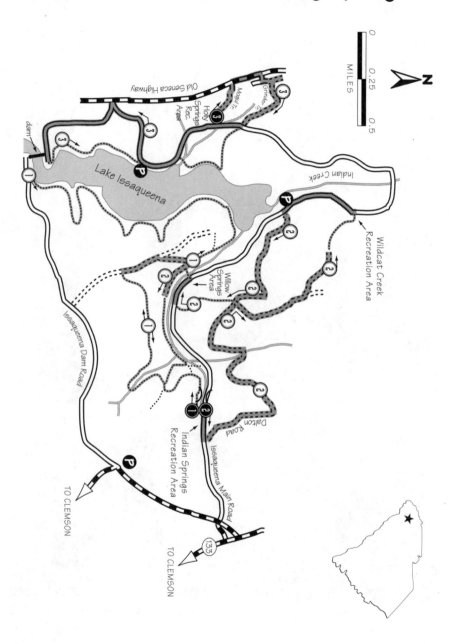

MILES

0   0.25   0.5

N

Old Seneca Highway

Holly Springs Rec. Area

Moori Tr.

Grinder Tr.

dam

Lake Issaqueena

Indian Creek

Wildcat Creek Recreation Area

Willow Springs Area

Issaqueena Dam Road

Indian Springs Recreation Area

Dalton Road

Issaqueena Main Road

TO CLEMSON

TO CLEMSON

133

Banking around a corner on sweet singletrack above Issaqueena Lake.
JOSHUA SCHAFFER PHOTO

0.0 Ride past the trailhead sign, head down a set of stone steps, and cross a bridge. Immediately reach a trail junction. Take the middle trail and follow Indian Creek downstream.

0.1 Stone steps lead down to the right; continue straight.

0.3 Cross a tributary on a stone bridge, then cross another on a wooden bridge.

0.5 At a trail junction, continue straight.

0.7 Ride through a small creek.

1.1 Pass by an open stand of pine, an example of Clemson's forestry projects.

1.4 Ride through a small creek.

1.5 Reach an old roadbed and travel right.

1.7 At a fork, go right and begin a short, rocky descent.

1.8 At the bottom, follow the somewhat hidden singletrack on the left.

2.0 At a fork, go right, traveling along Indian Creek again.

2.1 Reach Issaqueena Lake and enjoy traveling its eastern perimeter for almost 2 miles.

3.0 Ride across a wooden bridge.

3.5 Ride across another wooden bridge. The last 0.5 mile is dense with rhododendron and mountain laurel.

3.9 Reach Issaqueena Dam Road, turn around, and retrace your path to Indian Springs Recreation Area.

Dalton Road Ride

See Map on Page 15	

Location: 4 miles north of Clemson University in the Indian Springs Recreation Area at Issaqueena Lake.

Distance: 5-mile loop.

Tread: 1.9 miles on singletrack, 2.3 miles on old roadbed, and 0.8 mile on gravel road.

Aerobic level: Moderate; several long, gradual climbs.

Technical difficulty: 3-; two extremely steep descents and a challenging climb with waterbars rate a 3+.

Land status: Clemson University.

Maps: USGS Clemson, Six Mile; an inexpensive map from Sunshine Cycle in Clemson.

Access: Same as Ride 1.

Taking a break at Issaqueena Lake.

HIGHLIGHTS

Dalton Road, a well-maintained, closed forest road that consists of gravel, clay, and sand, is linked with several stretches of singletrack to create this 5-mile loop. You will travel half of Dalton Road at the beginning of your ride and the other half in the middle. The two steep downhill sections of singletrack—Technical Trail and Wounded Knee Trail—are sure to knock a screw loose.

This ride, which starts at Indian Springs Recreation Area, also travels through several other recreation areas at Issaqueena Lake: Wild Cat Creek and Willow Springs. Many local riders add Dalton Road to the Issaqueena Lake Trail for the ultimate workout. See the map for several possible connections.

THE RIDE

0.0 Go right out of the Indian Springs Recreation Area parking lot and head up Issaqueena Main Road.

0.1 Turn left on Dalton Road and ride around the cable. Enjoy mostly downhill to a tributary of Indian Creek.

0.9 Ride a bridge made of railroad ties across the creek and begin a short, gradual climb.

1.2 Pass a grassy field on your left and turn right at the intersection. Go up a short steep. This offshoot of Dalton Road soon narrows to singletrack.

1.6 At the Y intersection, fork right and begin riding down the singletrack trail called Technical.

1.9 The grade steepens.

2.2 Arrive at Wildcat Creek Recreation Area and go left. Be aware of people and cars in the parking lot.

2.3 Turn left onto Issaqueena Main Road.

2.8 Before a small parking area on the right, turn left and climb gradually on the other end of Dalton Road.

3.6 Arrive at an intersection (where you were at mile 1.2) and turn right onto the singletrack trail called Wounded Knee. Enjoy the whoop-dee-do's and sidehills on this exhilarating descent.

3.9 Turn right and ride Issaqueena Main Road to Willow Springs Recreation Area. Take the trail on the left across a bridge, then go left at the intersection, riding on a rocky old roadbed that becomes singletrack.

4.3 Cross a wet area.

4.4 Travel right at a T intersection and go up steeply on waterbars.

4.5 Another T intersection. Turn left, travel on good, level singletrack, riding across a wooden bridge, then a stone bridge. When steps lead off to the left, continue straight.

5.0 At an intersection (picnic table), go straight and up to the left to arrive back at Indian Springs Recreation Area.

Figure Eight at Holly Springs

See Map on Page 15

Location: 4 miles north of Clemson University in the Holly Springs Recreation Area at Issaqueena Lake.

Distance: 5.2-mile figure eight.

Tread: 1.5 miles on singletrack, 1.6 miles on old roadbed, 1.3 miles on gravel road, and 0.8 mile on pavement.

Aerobic level: Strenuous; a 0.5-mile gradual climb plus one short, super steep.

Technical difficulty: 2+; except the Dam Trail, which has a section of steps, and the new singletrack, which involves a steep, eroded climb and descent.

Land status: Clemson University.

Maps: USGS Clemson; an inexpensive map from Sunshine Cycle in Clemson.

Access: Follow access directions for Ride 1 to Indian Springs Recreation Area. Then continue another 2.8 miles to Holly Springs Recreation Area on the right. Park in front of the picnic shelter.

Along the Figure Eight at Holly Springs.

HIGHLIGHTS

The Figure Eight combines several short singletrack trails in the Holly Springs Recreation Area. The key word here is variety—to the extreme. You'll ride easy, then hard; flat, then steep. This ride is anything but consistent. Even the scenery changes drastically, from stark clearcut to beautiful lakeshore.

Begin with a steady 0.5-mile climb on the Mogul Trail. Then the Grinder Trail rewards you with a thrilling 1-mile descent, free of technical difficulties other than some loose rock and debris. Unfortunately, the Al Butt's Trail, which connected these two trails, was recently destroyed by a clearcut and you must ride pavement for a short distance.

A new trail across from the Holly Springs Recreation Area may be the toughest stretch of singletrack at Issaqueena. Too bad it's so short. And finally, the Dam Trail provides good, wooded singletrack along the lake and ends with a fun descent on stone steps.

THE RIDE

0.0 Go up the steps past the picnic shelter and locate the Mogul Trail, a clay roadbed that climbs through a recent clearcut.

0.4 Enter woods to the left; the trail soon levels off.

0.6 Reach a T intersection and travel right on pavement.

0.9 Turn left before the road deadends and ride around a cable. Turn right on Old

Seneca Highway.

1.1 Pass a road on the right blocked by two large tank traps. Continue a short distance to another road on the right and ride around a cable. Turn left and follow the paved road.

1.4 Pavement ends, fork right.

1.5 Fork right again and begin riding the Grinder Trail downhill.

2.4 Ride left around the cable and cross Issaqueena Main Road. Maneuver left around tank traps and begin riding downhill on singletrack.

2.8 Reach the banks of Issaqueena Lake at a good swimming spot. Locate an obscure trail on the right that follows the shoreline.

3.0 A challenging ascent, then an even more challenging descent to cross Holly Springs Creek.

3.1 Finish this stretch of singletrack with a short ascent to Issaqueena Main Road and turn left. Travel the gravel road alongside the lake and past a gravel parking lot.

3.6 Go left at the fork.

4.0 Arrive at the picnic area at the dam and ride one of three trails parallel to the shelter that come together to begin the Dam Trail.

4.5 At a confusing intersection of a number of trails, continue straight and ride down stone steps.

4.6 Ride down another set of steps, turn onto a wooden bridge, and head right to avoid more steps. At the paved footpath, go left.

4.8 Arrive at the gravel parking lot on Lake Issaqueena and turn right onto Issaqueena Main Road.

5.2 Return to Holly Springs Recreation Area.

Fants Grove Lake Trail

Location:	3 miles south of Clemson University, near the Seed Orchard Road at Fants Grove.
Distance:	4.3-mile loop.
Tread:	Singletrack with 1.4 miles on gravel and dirt road.
Aerobic level:	Moderate; short, rolling hills with one steep climb.
Technical difficulty:	3; rutted hills, exposed roots, tight turns, and drop-offs to the lake.
Land status:	Clemson University.
Maps:	USGS Clemson; an inexpensive map from Sunshine Cycle in Clemson.
Access:	From the intersection of U.S.Highway 123 and South Carolina 133 in Clemson, head south on SC 133 (College Avenue) for 0.5 mile to downtown and campus. At the traffic light, take a left onto SC 93. At the second traffic light, turn right onto South Palmetto Boulevard. Go straight through a three-way

Fants Grove Lake Trail •
Quarry Trail • Swine Farm Trail •
Johnstone Trail • Fox Trail

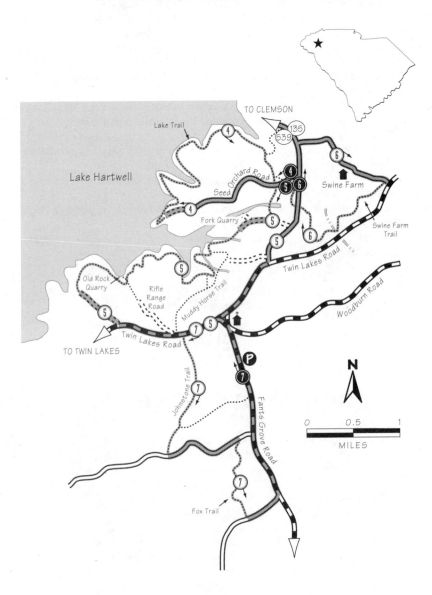

stop, then a four-way stop, and then a traffic light (Perimeter Road). Travel 0.7 mile (now Cherry Road) and turn right onto Old Cherry Road. Take the first left onto Fants Grove Road, after about 0.5 mile. You will cross railroad tracks and pass a coal yard. The small parking area at Seed Orchard Road is 1.2 miles farther on the right.

Highlights

Follow the shoreline of Lake Hartwell in and out of several wooded coves on this short, technical loop. Seed Orchard Road takes you down to a point on Lake Hartwell. Take a swim before you begin the scenic singletrack along the lake.

Erosion, overuse, and horse traffic on the singletrack will sharpen your technical skills, and the gentle rolling hills are just enough to keep you pumped. Finish with a bit of a push back up to the gravel road. The lake trail is the local favorite at Fants Grove.

The Ride

0.0 Ride down the gravel Seed Orchard Road.
0.5 Take the left fork, continuing down Seed Orchard Road, which eventually becomes dirt.
1.2 The road narrows to singletrack.
1.3 Reach the point on Lake Hartwell and enjoy the view. Then turn around, locate the Lake Trail on your left, and begin riding along the shore.
1.6 Enter the first cove on the ride.
2.4 Reach the second and largest cove. Negotiate a steep descent and cross a bridge.
2.6 The waves along the lake lap at the trail's edge.
3.2 Enter the final cove.
3.6 Trail junction. Go right to finish the loop.
4.0 Another trail junction, continue straight.
4.1 Reach the gravel road and go left.
4.3 Arrive back at the parking area on Seed Orchard Road.

Ian Davidson enjoys a doubletrack trail in the Clemson Experimental Forest.
Joshua Schaffer Photo

Quarry Trail

<table>
<tr><td rowspan="1">See Map
on Page 22</td><td>Location:</td><td>3 miles south of Clemson University, near the Seed Orchard Road at Fants Grove.</td></tr>
<tr><td>Distance:</td><td>5.9-mile loop.</td></tr>
<tr><td>Tread:</td><td>2.9 miles on singletrack, 1 mile on old roadbed, 0.2 mile on gravel road, and 1.8 miles on pavement.</td></tr>
<tr><td>Aerobic level:</td><td>Strenuous; a lot of short, steep climbs.</td></tr>
<tr><td>Technical difficulty:</td><td>3+; tight turns, log jumps, eroded steeps, roots and rocks, drop-offs to the lake, and a possible muddy section.</td></tr>
<tr><td>Land status:</td><td>Clemson University.</td></tr>
<tr><td>Maps:</td><td>USGS Clemson; an inexpensive map from Sunshine Cycle in Clemson.</td></tr>
<tr><td>Access:</td><td>Same as Ride 4.</td></tr>
</table>

HIGHLIGHTS

Like Fants Grove Lake Trail, this ride follows the shoreline of Lake Hartwell in and out of wooded coves. Be prepared for a more difficult ride with terribly eroded steeps. Beginner and intermediate riders will be off the bike frequently.

On the Quarry Trail, you will be rewarded with a longer ride and more scenic views across the lake. On a clear day, you can see the rolling foothills of the western part of the state.

THE RIDE

0.0 Head down the gravel Seed Orchard Road.

0.2 Turn left into the woods and head downhill on singletrack.

0.5 Ride through a small creek, then across a bridge of railroad ties. Begin an extremely technical climb.

0.8 At the T intersection, turn right onto a clay roadbed, which shows signs of heavy horse use. (If it is wet, cling to the pine trees and carry.)

1.1 Begin riding singletrack again. Cross a creek in the first lake cove of the ride.

1.3 Take the right fork. Cross a creek at the second cove. Begin riding along Lake Hartwell.

1.8 Enter the third cove and negotiate a difficult creek crossing on boulders. After leaving the lakeshore, begin a stretch of short steeps and confusing intersections. Go right at the T intersection and continue straight when a trail comes in on the left.

Carrying across a waterfall in Clemson Experimental Forest. JOSHUA SCHAFFER PHOTO

2.1 Back out on the water, enjoy views, across the lake, of the foothills.

2.9 At the T intersection, go right (not the extreme right turn, which leads to a point and the site of the Old Rock Quarry). Note: To shorten the ride, take the old roadbed to the left (Rifle Range Road).

3.0 Continue straight.

3.4 Enter the last cove of the ride, then climb gently from the lake on an old roadbed.

4.0 Reach a cul-de-sac and follow the sandy roadbed to the left.

4.1 Go right over a tank trap to the pavement and turn left.

4.8 Continue straight past the turn for Fants Grove Church.

5.2 Take the road to the left at the Y intersection.

5.9 Return to the parking area on Seed Orchard Road.

Swine Farm Trail

<table>
<tr><td rowspan="2" align="center">See Map
on Page 22</td><td align="right">**Location:**</td><td>3 miles south of Clemson University, near the Seed Orchard Road at Fants Grove.</td></tr>
<tr><td align="right">**Distance:**</td><td>2.6-mile loop.</td></tr>
<tr><td></td><td align="right">**Tread:**</td><td>1.6 miles on singletrack, 0.7 mile on gravel, and 0.3 mile on pavement.</td></tr>
<tr><td></td><td align="right">**Aerobic level:**</td><td>Moderate; rolling hills.</td></tr>
<tr><td></td><td align="right">**Technical difficulty:**</td><td>2; tree roots, loose rock, and other minor obstacles.</td></tr>
<tr><td></td><td align="right">**Land status:**</td><td>Clemson University.</td></tr>
<tr><td></td><td align="right">**Maps:**</td><td>USGS Clemson; an inexpensive map from Sunshine Cycle in Clemson.</td></tr>
<tr><td></td><td align="right">**Access:**</td><td>Same as Ride 4.</td></tr>
</table>

HIGHLIGHTS

This loop is great by itself, but most local riders add it to other trails at Fants Grove. See the map for a side trail that makes a connection to Fants Grove Lake Trail, and note the loop's proximity to the Quarry Trail.

This singletrack is not as difficult as some of the rides in the experimental forest. Use the Swine Farm Trail as a warm-up before heading out on a longer ride. There is one major creek crossing that usually must be crossed on downed trees.

THE RIDE

0.0 Turn left on the pavement, riding back toward Clemson.

0.3 Turn right onto the gravel road at the sign for Starkley's Swine Farm.

1.0 Locate the singletrack Swine Farm Trail on the right at the telephone pole and begin with an easy climb.

1.7 Several trails come in from the left; continue straight.

1.8 Reach a difficult creek crossing. Try downstream, carrying your bike across on some large fallen trees.

2.2 Take the left fork and ride across a bridge of railroad ties.

2.3 Cross the pavement and stay right.

2.6 Arrive back at the parking area on Seed Orchard Road.

YEEHAW!!!

Johnstone Trail and Fox Trail

See Map on Page 22

Location: 3 miles south of Clemson at Fants Grove, near the Fants Grove Church.

Distance: 4.3-mile loop.

Tread: 1.9 miles on singletrack, 1.2 miles on gravel road, and 1.2 miles on pavement.

Aerobic level: Moderate; rolling with a few steep climbs.

Technical difficulty: 3+; narrow track, rutted hills, log jumps, eroded sections, and a tight switchback.

Land status: Clemson University.

Maps: USGS Clemson, La France; an inexpensive map from Sunshine Cycle in Clemson.

Access: See Ride 4 directions to Seed Orchard Road. Continue 0.7 mile and turn right at the stop sign. After another 0.4 mile, turn left toward Fants Grove Church. At the intersection near the church, continue straight for another 0.3 mile and turn left into the large gravel parking lot.

HIGHLIGHTS

You can access a network of trails at Fants Grove from this new parking lot on Fants Grove Road, just past the church. This ride details two short singletrack trails in the area—Johnstone Trail and Fox Trail—leaving the others to be explored by riders who have some time and a sense of adventure. Pick up a map of Fants Grove from Sunshine Cycle and explore the other trails in the area.

Johnstone Trail and Fox Trail offer an introduction to this part of the experimental forest. This is just down-and-dirty trail riding in the woods. The loop provides equal amounts of singletrack, gravel road cruising, and pavement. While the singletrack may be short, it is worth checking out for its demanding technical challenges.

THE RIDE

0.0 Turn right on the pavement and return to Fants Grove Church.
0.3 Turn left at the church.
0.4 Turn left again at the next stop sign.
0.7 Reach the western trailhead for Johnstone Trail on the left. Take it.

1.6   Go right at the Y intersection.

1.7   Reach a gravel road and turn left.

2.4   Locate the singletrack Fox Trail on the right and begin a tricky descent.

2.7   Negotiate an ascending switchback followed by log jumps.

3.0   Stay left.

3.2   Reach a timber cut and take the trail left, straight across the clearcut.

3.3   Turn left on the gravel road, and turn left again when you reach the main gravel road.

3.8   Turn left when you reach the pavement of Fants Grove Road.

4.3   Return to the parking lot on the right via Fants Grove Road.

Timmons Park

The 26-acre Timmons Park, located in the city of Greenville, is home to the shortest mountain biking loop in the state, at least to my knowledge. And amazingly enough, this 1.8-mile urban trail offers a wide variety of riding conditions and terrain.

In addition to the trail, enjoy the shade and creekside picnicking at this well-kept park. Facilities include a tennis court, basketball court, ball field, playground, and restroom. Helmets are required at this city park. For more information, contact Greenville Parks and Recreation or the Greenville Spinners, the local bicycle club that sponsors the trail (see appendices A and C).

Timmons Park Mountain Bike Trail

Location:	2 miles east of downtown Greenville.
Distance:	1.8-mile loop.
Tread:	Singletrack.
Aerobic level:	Moderate; some very short hills.
Technical difficulty:	3; short, eroded steeps, technical descents, and tight trail with rocks and roots.
Land status:	Greenville city park.
Map:	USGS Greenville.
Access:	Take Exit 42 off Interstate 385, just west of downtown Greenville. Travel north on Stone Avenue. Immediately turn right on East North Street and go about 1 mile. After the school, look for a sign on the left for Timmons Park. Turn left on Blackburn Street, travel 0.3 mile, and take a sharp right turn into the park. Circle a little over halfway around the loop and park near the basketball court.

Highlights

The Greenville Spinners built this trail with the intent of having a practice ground close to home for after-work and lunch-hour workouts. Most locals use the trail on weekdays, riding the loop three or four times to keep their technical skills honed for weekend adventures.

Timmons Park Mountain Bike Trail

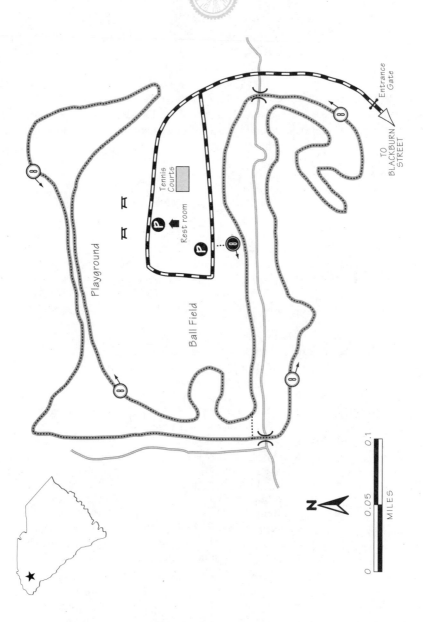

The small space the park offers has been utilized to its full potential. You have to see this trail to believe it. Be prepared for tight turns, rocks, and roots, a series of switchbacks, and some whoop-dee-do's. And with an elevation change of about 100 feet, the trail generates several short steeps and technical descents. Yes, all this in under 2 miles.

THE RIDE

0.0 Ride down, past a bike trail sign alongside some wooded steps, and head right on the singletrack by the creek.

0.1 At a Y intersection, veer hard to the right.

0.3 Climb slightly and ride past a pair of swing sets.

0.4 Turn left into the woods.

0.6 Come out at a swing set and turn right. Watch for a hard right to pick up the lower trail.

0.8 Back at the Y intersection, continue straight.

0.9 Cross a wooden bridge and continue straight.

1.0 Take the right fork for a short climb and technical descent, or go left for an easier route.

1.2 At the grassy area, turn right into the woods past a bike trail sign. Climb a short hill and go right down a difficult descent.

1.3 Begin ascending on several switchbacks.

1.5 Enter a grassy field. Cross through the middle to a high point and ride down toward the pavement. Then the trail goes around to the left.

1.6 Go right over a bridge.

1.8 Finish back at the wooden steps.

Paris Mountain State Park

Paris Mountain, a prominent natural landmark in Greenville, lies just north of downtown. The Cherokee Indians gave the mountain to Richard Pearis, the first white settler in the area. Pearis was famous for his friendly trading with the Cherokee. He married a Native American and started a family here.

The Civilian Conservation Corps developed the area in the mid 1930s after the state acquired the 1,275 acres from the city; the park opened in 1937. Because this tract of land is one of oldest protected areas in state, safe from development since 1890, the park contains some very large trees. The park once claimed the state record pine, which has since died. Expect to see beautiful stands of poplar, maple, oak, and pine along your ride.

In addition to the bike trail, the park offers a picnic area and campground, seasonal swimming in the 2-acre Lake Placid, and several hiking trails. A $2 user fee is charged per vehicle on weekends in the spring and fall, and daily in the summer. For more information, contact Paris Mountain State Park.

Firetower Trail

Location:	About 5 miles north of Greenville.
Distance:	3.2 miles out and back.
Tread:	Wide old roadbed.
Aerobic level:	Strenuous; gradual climb for half of the ride.
Technical difficulty:	2-; rocks, branches, and other minor obstacles.
Land status:	Paris Mountain State Park.
Maps:	USGS Paris Mountain, Taylors; a map is available from the state park.
Access:	Travel north on U.S. Highway 276 out of Greenville. Go east on South Carolina 253 for 2.5 miles and turn left onto State Park Road. The park entrance is on the left after 0.7 mile. Continue 2.5 miles through the park to a black gate and park on the left side of the cul-de-sac. Do not block the gate.

Firetower Trail

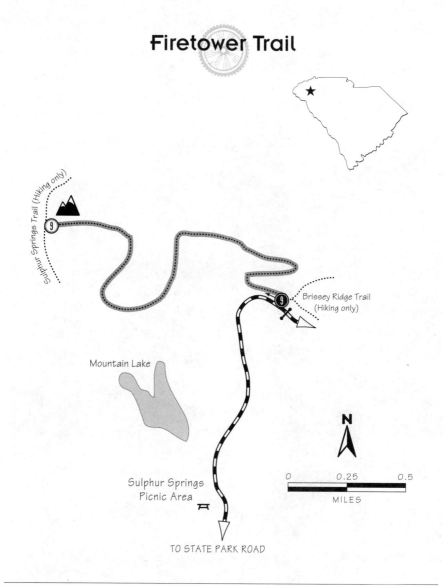

Sulphur Springs Trail (Hiking only)

Brissey Ridge Trail (Hiking only)

Mountain Lake

Sulphur Springs
Picnic Area

N

| 0 | | 0.25 | | 0.5 |

MILES

TO STATE PARK ROAD

HIGHLIGHTS

Traveling on an old firetower road, you will climb from the trailhead (elevation 1,555 feet) to the top of Paris Mountain (1,978 feet). There is no longer a firetower on the summit, only the abandoned foundation of the caretaker's house.

Most mountain bikers come to Paris Mountain for the workout. The climb is the major challenge on this wide roadbed, but keep an eye out for ruts, rocks, and debris. You won't be rewarded with a view from the summit (the trees are too thick), but there are several winter views from the trail, and the mountain laurel lining the road is beautiful in the spring.

Looking across the terrain of the Sumter National Forest to the majestic foothills of the Blue Ridge Mountains.

THE RIDE

0.0   The trailhead is on the left side of the cul-de-sac, opposite the gate. Begin traveling up the old firetower road.

0.5   At the time of publication, this was about as far as you could ride because of the damage from the ice storm.

1.6   Reach the summit of Paris Mountain and the intersection with Sulphur Springs Trail. Turn around and descend to the parking area.

Southside Park

Southside Park, a county-owned facility primarily used by ball players, now draws mountain bikers from around the Upstate. The trailhead is at the county's ballpark, but most of the trail is actually in Croft State Park. Tour de Dump was built as a race course, but at the time, there wasn't enough interest to keep the trail open.

During the past few years, local riders took it upon themselves to maintain the trail and are now working with the county to improve the quality. There seems to be a lack of coordination between mountain bikers and state officials. Croft State park does not recognize this area as an official state park trail.

But with the new parking lot completed, Southside mountain bikers are ready to correctly map all of the trail, put gravel in the low-lying areas, and build bridges for some of the creek crossings. Eventually, a new section of trail may be cut to avoid the powerline, which is not shaded and is super hot in the summer.

So while the county, the state park, and the local riders try to decide the future of Tour de Dump, folks are continuing to ride on this great trail. For more information, contact Croft State Park. The Great Escape, a bicycle shop in Spartanburg, may also be able to provide some details about the ride.

If you need a place to camp, facilities are available at Croft State Park, which served as a training camp for all phases of infantry combatants during World War II. After the war, the state purchased 7,088 acres from the federal government for a park. In addition to two camping areas, the state park offers hiking, picnicking, swimming, and tennis.

Bonus trail: Southside Park accesses two longer loops. For a few more climbs and some extra mileage, go left at mile 4.5 on the green-blazed trail, then take a right at the next junction for the second loop or continue straight for the third and longest loop.

Tour de Dump

Location:	15 miles south of Spartanburg at the southern end of Croft State Park.
Distance:	5.6-mile loop.
Tread:	Singletrack with 1.7 miles along powerline.
Aerobic level:	Strenuous; the hills along the powerline section are the steepest on the ride.
Technical difficulty:	3; tight turns, creek crossings, and slippery, steep hills.
Land status:	County park and state park.

Tour de Dump

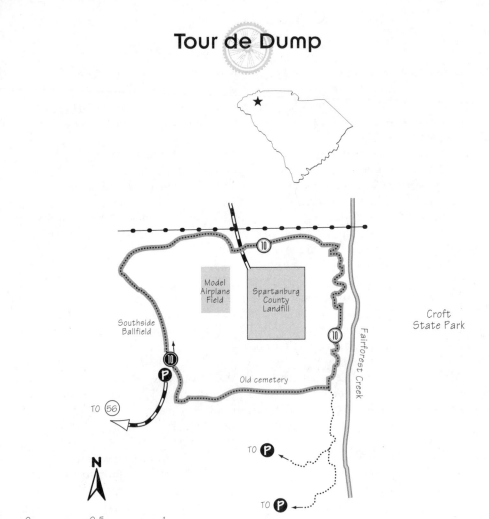

Maps: USGS Pacolet, Glen Springs; the information board at the parking area has map and trail descriptions.

Access: From Interstate 85 west of Spartanville, take Exit 63 and turn right onto South Carolina 290. Reach SC 296 and turn left onto SC 295, then turn right. Follow signs to the park, heading south on SC 56 toward Pauline. Pass the entrance to Croft State Park, travel about 3 miles, and turn left on Groce Road. Follow this road, taking the right (or straight) fork, to the Southside Ballfield.

Highlights

The parking lot at Southside has been packed recently. The main loop is well marked with orange blazes and circles one of the county's landfills.

This ride begins along a powerline cut, but soon enters a pine-hardwood forest on sandy singletrack and follows Fairforest Creek for 2.3 miles. Toward the end of the ride, you will pass an old family cemetery that dates back to the 1850s.

The challenges include rolling ups and downs, mudholes, creek crossings, and exciting berms on several of the turns. Tour de Dump is singletrack except for the section of wide red clay along the powerline, which adds a hard workout on some extremely hilly terrain. This section has no shade and can be hot in the summer.

Note: There is a very dangerous downhill about 200 yards after crossing the paved road (mile 0.8). Approach this drop-off with caution. The line constantly changes.

The Ride

0.0 Ride alongside the ballfield and past the information board on the right.

0.2 Enter the woods about halfway around the ballfield. Get ready for 0.1 mile of steep, muddy, narrow trail.

0.3 Reach the powerline section of the ride.

0.8 Cross a paved road and begin riding the powerline again.

1.5 At a fork, take a left to stay on the main trail. The right fork shortens the loop by about 0.75 mile.

1.7 At the top of the hill, take a sharp right into the woods and begin singletrack.

2.0 First view of Fairforest Creek.

2.2 Trail junction. The yellow-blazed trail is a short cut.

2.5 Ford a small tributary.

2.7 Ride along Fairforest Creek again.

3.5 Cross a ditch on a narrow metal catwalk. Be careful.

4.1 Ford another small tributary.

4.5 Turn right to finish this loop. (The green-blazed trail to the left leads to two longer loops.)

4.8 Pass old family cemetery on the right.

5.6 Return to the ballfield parking lot.

The Piedmont

The rolling terrain of the Piedmont comprises the largest region of the state. Elevations range from 400 to 1,000 feet. This is a land of pine forests, fertile pastures, and large lakes. Much of the Piedmont is thoroughbred country; the weather is perfect for breeding and training top racehorses.

Columbia, the capital city, is located in the geographic center of the state and acts as a hub for financial, social, and educational activity in South Carolina. This contemporary city with its historic remnants offers excellent museums, a lively art scene, and many cultural events.

A rest day could be well spent at Columbia's 50-acre Riverbanks Zoo along the Saluda River. The zoo is known for its success in breeding endangered species. Over 2,000 animals from jungle, ocean, and desert environments live here in their natural habitats. Highlights include a rain forest exhibit and a typical southern farm. Or, visit the South Carolina State Museum, which interprets history, art, science, and geology in a four-story renovated textile mill. Shopping and eating are great in the Five Points district.

The eastern edge of the Piedmont is called the Sandhills, where an ancient sea created hills of sand that rise up to 600 feet. You get the feeling that you are nearing the coast, but mountain laurel and rhododendron remind you that you are on the border of the Piedmont. Two state forests—Manchester and Sand Hills—offer great roller coaster–type mountain bike rides.

The western edge of the Piedmont contains a good number of mountain bike trails, mostly within the national forest around McCormick. The folks in the area are working hard to make this the "mountain bike mecca" of South Carolina. My favorite trails are along the dark, slow-moving waters of Turkey and Steven's creeks, where you ride on high bluffs above the river, and ferns and galax cover the ground.

The Piedmont is home to many large lakes. One of the nation's largest, Lake Thurmond, was created in 1954 when the waters of the Savannah were impounded. This 40-mile-long body of water is located on the western border of the Long Cane Ranger District of Sumter National Forest. Other large lakes include Lake Marion and Lake Moultrie. Fishing is big in this area, probably because the bass, crappie, and brim are big, too. You'll find many lakeside communities that cater to anglers.

For more information about the Piedmont, call the Columbia Metropolitan Convention and Visitors Bureau, the Santee-Cooper Counties Promotion Commission, and the McCormick County Chamber of Commerce (see Appendix A). Welcome centers are located as you enter the state from North Carolina on Interstate 77 and I-95, as well as from Georgia on I-20 and U.S. Highway 301.

Anne Springs Close Greenway

Anne Springs Close Greenway, a gift to the public from the eight Close children, forms an arc around the northern portion of Fort Mill and provides a 2,000-acre natural recreation area for residents and visitors. The children inherited the property from their grandfather Colonel Elliot White Springs in 1959. Their contribution to the community honors their mother, Anne, a nature lover and dedicated conservationist.

Of the 26 miles of trail, bicycles are allowed on designated trails north of Steele Creek and east of U.S. Highway 21 (business). Obtain a map of the greenway from the Nature Center. A nominal entrance fee is charged to help with operation costs (children 6 years old and under are admitted free). Annual memberships are available for residents and people who work full-time in the area. Please consider making a contribution to Friends of the Greenway. For more information, contact Anne Springs Close Greenway (see Appendix A).

Bonus trail: While you are in the area, go by College Cycles in Rock Hill and talk with Robert Baker to find out about 7 miles of mountain bike trail on nearby private land. This family-owned trail is generally referred to as McConnell's.

Springfield Loop

Location:	About 8 miles east of Rock Hill.
Distance:	3.3-mile loop and an optional 2.2-mile out-and-back.
Tread:	Singletrack with 0.6 mile on gravel road.
Aerobic level:	Moderate; a 1-mile stretch of short ups and downs.
Technical difficulty:	2 + ; short steeps, technical descents, and difficult creek crossings rate a 3.
Land status:	Anne Springs Close Greenway.
Maps:	USGS Fort Mill; a map of all the trails in the Anne Springs Close Greenway is available from the Nature Center.
Access:	Go about 6 miles north from Rock Hill on Interstate 77 to South Carolina 160. Take SC 160 east toward Fort Mill. Cross U.S. Bypass 21 and travel 0.7 mile to U.S. Highway (business) 21. Turn left and travel about 2.5 miles to the Dairy Barn entrance (Springfield Lane). Turn left onto the gravel road. The parking lot and self-service fee station are 0.3 mile, on the left.

Springfield Loop

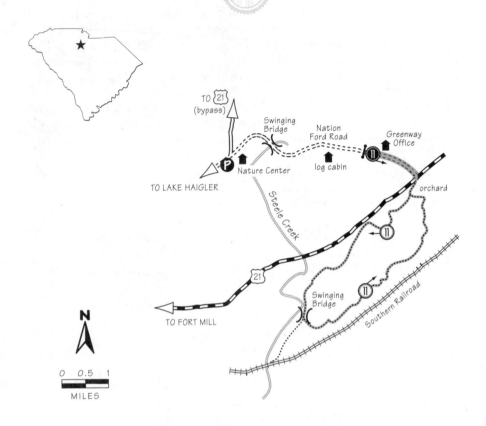

TO [21] (bypass)

Swinging Bridge

Nation Ford Road

Greenway Office

P

Nature Center

log cabin

TO LAKE HAIGLER

orchard

Steele Creek

[21]

TO FORT MILL

Swinging Bridge

Southern Railroad

N

0   0.5   1
MILES

HIGHLIGHTS

Springfield Loop packs a lot of punch in its 3.3 miles. The back side of the loop includes short steeps, technical descents, and difficult creek crossings. You will ride through upland forest, including pignut hickory, short-leaf pine, sourwood, and dogwood. Highlights include a swinging bridge and several log jumps.

For a quick warm-up before hitting the loop, ride along the historic Nation Ford Road, past a restored 1785 log cabin, to the Nature Center (0.8 mile), and return. This early Indian trading path, often called the Great Wagon Road, ran from Pennsylvania south to Charles Town (now Charleston).

Note: Mountain bikers are not allowed on trails in the Nation Ford Road area except on the gravel road. Also, to the Springfield Loop you can add the short extension out to Steele Creek, which connects to several loops of horse trail that can be ridden if conditions permit.

Biking in upland forest country.

THE RIDE

0.0 Ride back out a gravel road (or go left and around a gate if you want to ride Nation Ford Road first).

0.3 Pass the Greenway Office and cross US Business 21. Ride along an orchard, then follow the trail signs left to locate the wooded singletrack.

0.6 At a fork, take a right to ride the loop counterclockwise.

1.5 After the swinging bridge, take a sharp left to continue on the loop. (Or go straight and ride through hardwood bottoms out to Steele Creek. After 0.3 mile, reach a railroad trestle and return.)

1.6 Begin the 1-mile stretch of ups and downs.

2.7 At the trail junction, go right and retrace the first 0.6 mile of the ride.

3.0 Return to US Business 21.

3.3 Arrive back at the parking lot.

Enoree Ranger District of Sumter National Forest

About 45 miles northwest of Columbia, the Enoree Ranger District of Sumter National Forest covers 160,000 acres of pine-hardwood forest typical of the rolling Piedmont country. Three large rivers run through the district: the Broad, the Enoree, and the Tyger.

The area has always been popular with equestrians, ATVs, and motorcycles, but recently the Forest Service has seen an increase in mountain bikers. Bikers are welcome to ride on the forest's 31 miles of horse trail and 19 miles of off-highway vehicle trail.

The Brickhouse Campground, convenient to both trailheads, serves trail users from late spring to early winter. The campground was named for its proximity to the Brickhouse at the junction of South Carolina 66 and State Route 276. This large, two-story house, built in the early 1800s, was once used as a stagecoach stop.

When considering a ride on national forest land, always be sure to check the dates of hunting season, which change from year to year. The Forest Service recommends avoiding the Enoree district from October through December—except on Sundays, when mountain bikers can safely enjoy the national forest trails because hunting is prohibited.

Bonus trail: In addition to the two long trails included in this section, Sumter's Woods Ferry Recreation Area offers three equestrian trails totaling 9 miles. For more information, contact the Enoree Ranger District of Sumter National Forest (see Appendix A).

Enoree Off-Highway Vehicle Trail

Location:	10 miles east of Clinton.
Distance:	4-mile loop.
Tread:	Singletrack with 1 mile on old roadbed.
Aerobic level:	Moderate; rolling hills.
Technical difficulty:	2; a few sections with mudholes and soft sand.
Land status:	Enoree Ranger District of Sumter National Forest.
Maps:	USGS Newberry West; a map including all five loops is available from the Forest Service.
Access:	From Clinton, travel south on Interstate 26 about 5 miles to Exit 60 and go east on South Carolina 66. Travel 3.7 miles and turn left on Stomp Springs Road

Enoree Off-Highway Vehicle Trail

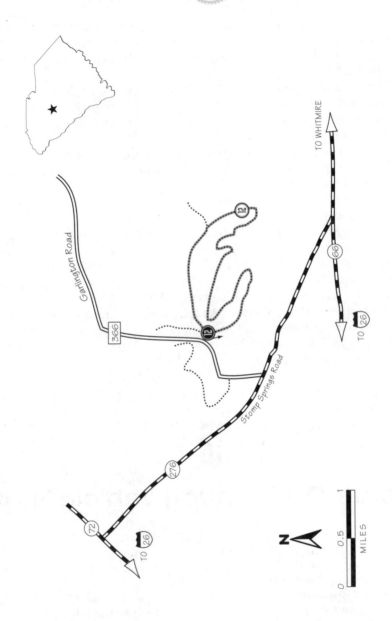

(State Route 276). After another 2.3 miles, turn right on Garlington Road (Forest Road 366). The parking lot is 0.3 mile on the right.

Highlights

This ride is one of five interconnecting loops called the Enoree Off-Highway Vehicle Trail. A rough sketch of the complete route, distributed by the Forest Service, gives you another 15 miles to explore. While designed for motorcycles and ATVs, the trail sees little use on weekdays.

This loop takes you up and down several times on gently rolling hills, and the smooth trail lets you ride fast. The motorcycles have created fun berms, whoop-dee-do's, and mudholes. You will find few obstacles, and the hard-packed sand remains in good shape except after a big rain.

When I rode at Enoree, a portion of the trail was closed for repair, which is sometimes the case there when loops are rerouted. The description here completes Loop 1 using a clay roadbed.

The Upstate Trail Riders Association, a motorcycle club which supports mountain bike use at Enoree, works with the Forest Service to maintain the five loops. Contact the Forest Service to find out about scheduled workdays.

The Ride

0.0 Looking toward the back of the large parking area, take the trail (with the arrow) on the far right and follow the gray diamonds.

1.1 The trail swings back by the parking area. Begin a fast 0.5-mile descent.

3.0 Reach a T intersection. The loop is closed to the right. Follow the clay roadbed left (yellow blazes).

3.5 At another trail junction, turn left.

4.0 Return to the parking area.

Negotiating mudholes on the Enoree Off-Highway Vehicle Trail.

Buncombe Trail

Location:	10 miles east of Clinton.
Distance:	9.1 miles one way.
Tread:	Singletrack with some wide roadbed and 1.8 miles on gravel road.
Aerobic level:	Strenuous; rolling hills and several long climbs.
Technical difficulty:	3; narrow trail, creek crossings, soft sand, and short bumpy sections (muddy when wet!).
Land status:	Enoree Ranger District of Sumter National Forest.
Maps:	USGS Newberry West; a map of the trail is available from the Forest Service.
Access:	From Clinton, travel south on Interstate 26 about 5 miles to Exit 60 and go east on South Carolina 66. Travel 3.7 miles and turn right onto Brickhouse Road (Forest Road 358). The parking lot is 0.2 mile on the left. (To park a second vehicle at the terminus of the trail, turn right on Crommer Road/FR 356, the next right after Brickhouse Road. Travel 2.3 miles and fork right onto Ponds Road/FR 361. After another 3 miles, park on the right at FR 359.)

HIGHLIGHTS

The Palmetto Trail uses this section of the Buncombe Trail to cross the Sumter Passage. The passage will eventually traverse the southern half of the ranger district. Enjoy this 9.1-mile ride, and if you liked this stretch, come back and explore the rest of the Buncombe Trail. See the map for details on the entire loop.

This section of the equestrian loop is in fairly good shape, and only short stretches of the hard-packed clay are torn up from horse traffic. Otherwise, you'll find excellent singletrack along pine ridges and through hardwood bottoms. Be prepared for several creek crossings. The Union County Horse Association maintains the first 2 miles of trail; after that, the white blazes can occasionally be hard to follow.

THE RIDE

0.0 Head left down the gravel FR 358.
0.2 Just before the campground, pick up the singletrack on the right and begin a 0.5-mile descent.

Buncombe Trail

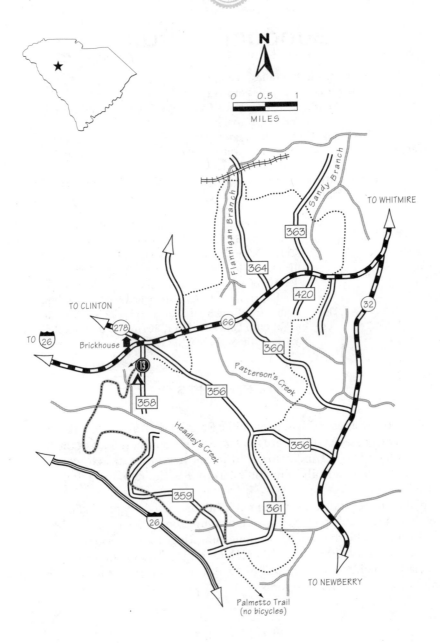

N

0   0.5   1

MILES

TO WHITMIRE

363

364

420

32

TO CLINTON

278

TO 26

Brickhouse

66

360

13

358

356

Patterson's Creek

Flannigan Branch

Sandy Branch

356

Headley's Creek

359

361

26

TO NEWBERRY

Palmetto Trail
(no bicycles)

0.7   Cross a bridge over Mulberry Branch.

1.0   Reach a recent clearcut and travel right on an old roadbed through a young pine forest.

1.4   The road narrows, veer left into woods onto singletrack.

1.9   Enjoy a fun descent with a long stretch of whoop-dee-do's.

2.1   Turn right and get ready for a good creek crossing. Tackle a section of soft sand on the other side of the creek and begin climbing on switchbacks.

2.4   Pass a mile marker that reads 2.

3.0   Take either fork but be sure to turn left when you hit the gravel road and then go around a red gate.

3.9   Reach a cul-de-sac at the end of the gravel-road descent and go left (not sharp left).

4.1   Cross a small creek and begin a gradual climb on a nice wooded section of trail.

4.7   Trail junction. Continue straight.

4.8   Follow the edge of a clearcut, right on a gravel road.

5.2   Travel around a wooden gate and immediately return to singletrack to the left. This stretch is very narrow.

5.3   Cross a gravel road and ride for another 0.5 mile on narrow trail with some briars.

5.8   Back to nice wooded trail.

6.2   Take a left at the T intersection and immediately cross a gravel road. Enjoy a hilly portion of the ride.

7.9   Cross a gravel road.

8.6   Turn right onto the gravel FR 359 and begin climbing.

9.1   Reach your shuttle vehicle at the junction on FR 361.

This section of the Buncombe Trail is now part of the cross-state Palmetto Trail.

Lynches Woods Park

Lynches Woods, a 276-acre tract of woodlands, creeks, and rolling hills, was originally part of a project by the Civilian Conservation Corps. This county-owned land has been popular with hikers and equestrians for years. Recently, the area was discovered by the mountain bikers of Newberry.

The mountain bike trail at Lynches Woods was the brain child of local riders Henry Mandrell and Rick Attaway. With help from friends and additional support from Cycle Center in Columbia, they flagged and mapped a route that is quickly becoming one of the more popular rides in the area.

The town hopes that Lynches Woods will be a major stop on the cross-state Palmetto Trail. They are planning to build primitive campsites and picnic shelters. The area is surrounded by private land, so getting the Palmetto Trail in and out is going to be a challenge.

For more information, contact Cycle Center in Columbia (see Appendix B).

Lynches Woods Bike Trail

Location:	Newberry, approximately 1 hour southeast from Greenville or northwest from Columbia.
Distance:	6.1-mile loop.
Tread:	Singletrack.
Aerobic level:	Moderate/difficult.
Technical difficulty:	3+.
Land status:	Managed by Newberry Soil and Water Conservation District.
Maps:	USGS Newberry East.
Access:	From Columbia, heading west on Interstate 26, take the first exit for Newberry and turn left onto South Carolina 219. Once in town, turn left at the Shell Station onto U.S. Highway 76 Bypass and go through a flashing light. At the Ford dealership, turn left on a dirt road. Park 400 yards down on the right.

Lynches Woods Bike Trail

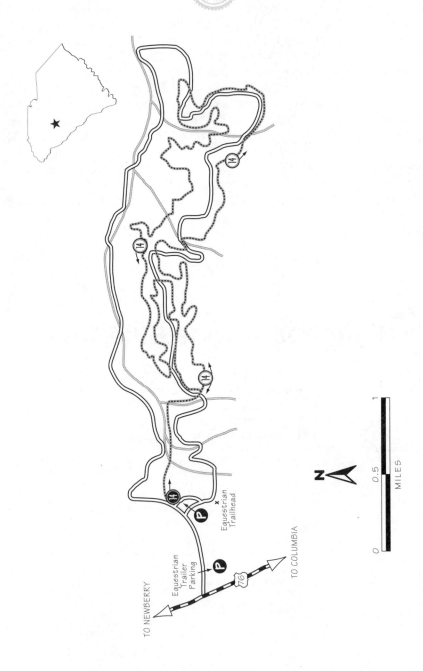

Map courtesy of Newberry Soil and Water Conservation District.

HIGHLIGHTS

This new trail is getting a lot of traffic out of Columbia. While there are horse trails in the area, this loop is designated for hikers and bikers only. The ride offers many technical challenges, taking the area's best bicyclists about 40 minutes to complete the 6.1 miles. You'll encounter several short hills and ride an interesting section in a ravine.

The trail crisscrosses the main dirt road of Lynches Woods several times. Use caution because there may be car traffic. This well-marked trail is blazed in orange.

THE RIDE

0.0 Pick up the entrance trail across from the main parking area.
0.4 Go straight across the road, then take the left fork to begin the main loop.
5.7 Cross a dirt road for the last time and retrace your tracks on the entrance trail.
6.1 Return to the parking area.

Long Cane Ranger District of Sumter National Forest

If you haven't heard about what's going on in McCormick County, in the heart of the Long Cane Ranger District of Sumter National Forest, it won't be long. Several groups have come together to promote the trails in the area, including plans to become the state's mountain bike mecca. With what's in the works, the area will soon have the highest concentration of mountain bike trails in the state. This is one of the first large-scale efforts involving mountain bikers in South Carolina.

The Mecca Trails Association (MTA) organized early in 1997 to bring agencies together in a collaborative effort to improve and market the recreational opportunities in the area. Members include land managers, trail users, chambers of commerce, and several county development boards.

The future looks bright for mountain biking in the area. The MTA recently received a $12,000 grant from the state to improve existing trails and build new trails in McCormick and Edgefield counties. The efforts at this time are concentrating on connecting Hamilton Branch State Park to Steven's Creek Trail in order to provide camping at the park with mountain biking in the national forest. Another major project involves a new trail at Baker Creek State Park, which is a perfect place to host races and festivals.

The town of McCormick provides mountain bikers with the basic amenities along with several bed-and-breakfasts and a historic 1880s hotel. Cyrus H. McCormick, Jr., the town's namesake and inventor of the McCormick reaper (a revolutionary agricultural implement), donated the land for a large portion of the town and planned its development with long narrow lots like his home city of Chicago. This rural town has several sites on the National Register of Historic Places and recent renovations have returned downtown to its early 1900s appearance.

The Long Cane ranger district covers about 120,000 acres in the west-central part of the state. Lake Thurmond, one of the largest lakes in the Southeast, offers 1,200 miles of shoreline, which is almost entirely national forest. There are four campgrounds run by the U.S. Army Corps of Engineers, or you can stay at one of three state parks—Hamilton Branch, Baker Creek, or Hickory Knob. Also, two Forest Service recreation areas—Parson's Mountain Lake and Horn Creek—serve the area with opportunities for camping, swimming, hiking, and picnicking. For more information, contact the Mecca Trails Association or the Long Cane Ranger District of Sumter National Forest. The office for the Lone Cane ranger district is located southeast of McCormick in the town of Edgefield (junction of U.S. Highway 25 and South Carolina 430).

Augusta Freewheelers, the local bicycle club, deserves high praise for their work on area trails and their involvement in the MTA. They adopted and continue to maintain three of the most popular trails in Sumter National Forest. This is a golden opportunity for cyclists to be leaders in trail advocacy issues. Please consider joining this organization. They are doing great things in the area and need your support (see Appendix C for more information).

Note: All the trails in this section are on national forest land. This ranger district is extremely popular with hunters, so it is a good idea to avoid riding here between October and December. Be sure to check on specific dates and regulations, which change from year to year.

Parson's Mountain Motorcycle Trail (Right Loop)

Location:	About 20 miles north of McCormick in Parson's Mountain Lake Recreation Area.
Distance:	7.6-mile loop.
Tread:	Singletrack with 0.3 mile on gravel road.
Aerobic level:	Strenuous; rolling with a couple steep climbs.
Technical difficulty:	3+; roots, loose gravel, mudholes, and rocky steeps. Trail conditions add to the rating.
Land status:	Long Cane Ranger District of the Sumter National Forest.
Maps:	USGS Verdery; a map with both loops is available from the Forest Service.
Access:	Travel north out of McCormick about 18 miles on U.S. Highway 28 toward Abbeville. After crossing into Abbeville County, continue 1.7 miles to Tower Road (Forest Road 515). Turn right and go another 0.3 mile to the parking area on the right. (To reach the recreation area, go back to US 28, head north, and turn right at the sign onto State Route 251. The entrance is 1.4 miles on the right.)

HIGHLIGHTS

My riding partner on this loop considered Parson's some of the best mountain biking in the state. Indeed, the rolling hills, berms, and whoop-dee-do's are great, but you must catch this trail when conditions are right or you'll be hub deep in mud. Parson's, designed for recreational motorcycles, was the site of the South Carolina State Mountain Bike Championships during the

Parson's Mountain Motorcycle Trail

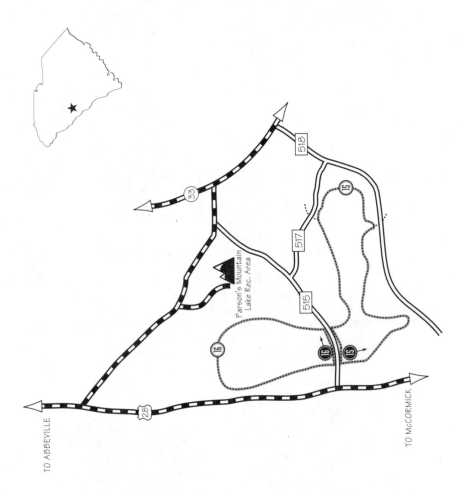

late 1980s and early 1990s. Quality trail exists, but an extended dry period along with a quiet weekday are essential for a good ride.

Part of the fun on a motorcycle trail is dodging the mudholes. Picking the best line will keep you on the bike. Other technical sections include steeps, roots, and loose rock. The bermed corners can be ridden particularly fast. After the ride, drive into the recreation area and take a swim.

THE RIDE

0.0 Head toward the back of the parking area past the information board and take the trail to the left. Note: Don't be discouraged by the rocky terrain. The trail improves after the first 0.25 mile.

0.5 Cross a small tributary on a wooden bridge.

1.0 Go left at a fork. A grassy road leads right.

2.1 Go left again and begin a section on red clay with large mudholes.

2.6 Begin riding a narrow, maintained gravel road.

3.4 Turn left at a trail sign and begin a tricky descent to a wooden bridge. Caution: On the last 30 yards, concrete blocks in the trail help prevent erosion.

4.2 Trail forks as you near a gravel road. Take either trail, they come back together shortly.

5.4 A trail comes in from the right; continue straight.

5.9 Work hard on the steepest hill of the ride.

7.3 Reach gravel Forest Road 515 and turn left to return to the parking lot.

7.6 Arrive back at the parking lot.

Parson's Mountain Motorcycle Trail (Left Loop)

See Map on Page 58	**Location:**	About 20 miles north of McCormick in Parson's Mountain Lake Recreation Area.
	Distance:	4.6-mile loop.
	Tread:	Singletrack with 0.3 mile on gravel road.
	Aerobic level:	Strenuous; two long climbs.
	Technical difficulty:	3; roots, loose rock, mudholes, eroded trail, and a difficult creek crossing.
	Land status:	Long Cane Ranger District of Sumter National Forest.
	Maps:	USGS Verdery; a map with both loops is available from the Forest Service.
	Access:	Same as Ride 15.

Relaxing at Parson's Mountain Lake.

HIGHLIGHTS

Combine this ride with the Right Loop for a total of 11.6 miles. You'll find longer, more gradual climbs along with exhilarating descents during the first few miles; the home stretch parallels U.S. Highway 28 and is flat cruising with lots of mudholes. The trail travels through hardwood bottoms, creek drainages, and pine plantations. See Highlights under Ride 15 for more specifics about riding this motorcycle trail.

THE RIDE

0.0 Travel right and up on gravel Forest Road 515.
0.3 Turn left on a dirt road and descend.
0.6 Veer left onto singletrack and descend for more than 0.5 mile.
1.2 Good creek crossing.
1.8 Cross a grassy road.
2.8 Hear vehicles as you begin riding near South Carolina 28.
3.3 Pass a small parking area at the gated FR 1961 on the left. Continue straight.
3.7 Cross a dirt road.
4.5 Turn left on the gravel FR 515.
4.6 Arrive back at the parking area on right.

Long Cane Horse Trail

Location:	About 20 miles north of McCormick in Parson's Mountain Lake Recreation Area.
Distance:	16.1-mile loop.
Tread:	Singletrack with 1.2 miles on gravel and 0.7 mile on pavement.
Aerobic level:	Strenuous; lots of hills.
Technical difficulty:	3; mudholes, soft sand, loose rock, and other debris—plus sections of churned-up, eroded trail from horse use.
Land status:	Long Cane Ranger District of Sumter National Forest.
Maps:	USGS Verdery, Abbeville East; a map is available from the Forest Service.

Long Cane Horse Trail

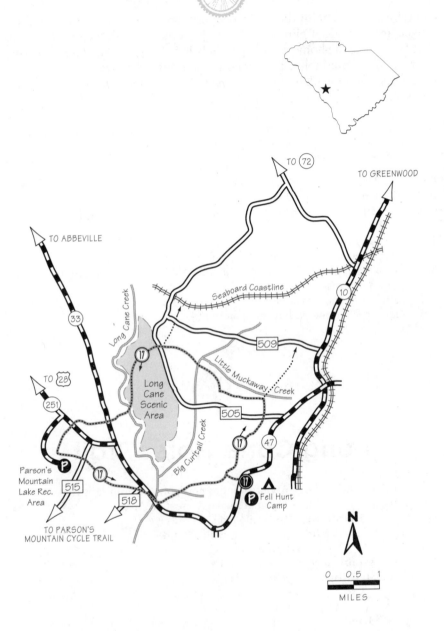

TO 72

TO GREENWOOD

TO ABBEVILLE

Seaboard Coastline

10

33

Long Cane Creek

509

TO 28

Little Muckaway Creek

251

Long
Cane
Scenic
Area

505

Big Curtail Creek

17

47

Parson's
Mountain
Lake Rec.
Area

P

515

17

518

17

P Fell Hunt
Camp

TO PARSON'S
MOUNTAIN CYCLE TRAIL

N

0   0.5   1

MILES

Access: About 2 miles west of Abbeville, at the junction of
          South Carolina 28/72, travel south on SC 28 for
          2.2 miles. Turn left onto State Route 251 and pass
          Parson's Mountain Lake Recreation Area on the right
          after 1.4 miles. Reach a three-way intersection after
          another 1.5 miles and turn right onto SR 33. In 2.8
          miles, take the left fork onto SC 47 and park at Fell
          Hunt Camp, which is 1.5 miles farther on the right.

HIGHLIGHTS

The Long Cane Horse Trail offers close to 25 miles of bridle path. Horses and mountain bikers don't always mix, but if you've often ridden Parson's Motorcycle Trail, a little exploring might be just the thing. Be forewarned, the hard-packed clay singletrack is often interrupted by stretches of muddy, churned-up, and overgrown trail, but I think this scenic adventure merits a trip.

Part of this ride traverses Long Cane Scenic Area, and while the riding is tough going at times, the beauty of the floodplain makes it well worth the effort. Long Cane Creek, which you cross once in the scenic area and again on paved State Route 33, takes its name from the bamboo-like plant growing along the banks. Other highlights include hardwood coves, old growth, and a couple of state record–size trees.

This ride, basically the southern half of the horse trail, uses the Connector Trail to create a 16.1-mile loop. Fell Hunt Camp serves as the trailhead, but you can also pick up the trail at Parson's Mountain Lake Recreation Area.

THE RIDE

0.0 Cross State Route 47 and locate a trailhead and large map across from Fell Hunt Camp.
0.7 Take a right fork to ride the loop counterclockwise.
1.8 Cross the gravel Forest Road 505.
2.2 Reach a three-way intersection and take a left to pick up what is called the Connector Trail.
2.5 The trail heads up away from the creek. Be sure to take the trail to the right.
3.1 Take a somewhat hidden right fork and cross a creek with the help of a fallen tree.
3.3 After the posted area off to the right, enjoy a stretch of good singletrack through a stand of pine.
3.5 Reach a petroleum pipeline cut, turn right, and ride up and down several hills.
4.0 Take your shoes off for a wet crossing of Big Curltail Creek.
4.1 Turn left into the woods onto singletrack.
4.5 Ride along a field and then cross Cedar Spring Motorcycle Trail.
5.2 Cross the gravel FR 505 and climb on water bars. You are now in the Long Cane Scenic Area.
5.5 Take a left fork.

The largest white oak in South Carolina is found along the Long Cane Horse Trail.

6.5 A trail comes in from the right; continue straight.

6.6 Reach a beautiful hardwood cove and the largest shagbark hickory tree in South Carolina (circumference: 10 feet, 6 inches; height: 135 feet).

7.4 Pass open woods and a great campsite.

7.7 Go right across Long Cane Creek on a metal bridge, or ride farther downstream to a deep ford. Once on the other side, take the right fork.

8.2 Enjoy the open floodplain area for 0.25 mile.

8.6 Fork left (not following the white blazes) for a better route through the low-lying area.

8.8 Cross the paved SR 33 and begin a gradual climb.

9.5 Cross the paved SR 251 and ride into Parson's Mountain Lake Recreation Area on an old roadbed.

10.0 Pass through a section of the campground.

10.4 Reach the gravel FR 515 and the largest white oak in South Carolina.

12.0 Reach the gravel FR 518 and turn left. At the junction with SR 33, turn right and ride on pavement.

12.7 Cross a bridge over Long Cane Creek and turn left off the pavement at the next pull-off to pick up the trail again.

13.2 Cross a bridge over Stillhouse Branch and begin riding on the gravel FR 537.

14.4 Reach the cul-de-sac at the end of gravel FR 537.

14.6 Begin a descent on an old roadbed to a tributary of Big Curltail Creek.

15.4 Look for the right turn that takes you back to Fell Hunt Camp.

16.1 Return to the parking area.

Turkey Creek Trail (South)

Location:	About 15 miles southeast of McCormick, south of Key Bridge on Turkey Creek.
Distance:	7.5 miles one way.
Tread:	Singletrack.
Aerobic level:	Moderate; rolling with several short climbs.
Technical difficulty:	3; wet crossings, switchbacks, and many bridges.
Land status:	Long Cane Ranger District of Sumter National Forest.
Maps:	USGS Parksville; a map is available from the Forest Service.
Access:	Travel about 9 miles south out of McCormick on U.S. Highway 221 to Parksville. Turn left onto South Carolina 138 at the sign for Price's Mill; you'll reach a stop sign after 4.8 miles. Turn right, travel 2.8 miles, and locate the trailhead on the right just before the steel Key Bridge. Park on the shoulder. (To set shuttle, park the second vehicle on Forest Road 617A. From Parksville, take SC 138 at the sign for Price's Mill, travel 2.5 miles, turn right onto a Forest Service road, then immediately fork right onto FR 617. Go 0.7 mile and turn right onto FR 617A, before the next fork. Park at the end of the road, another 0.7 mile.)

Highlights

Come ride the banks of Turkey and Steven's creeks. Much of the time, this shaded trail follows the bluff just above the water; occasionally, the trail leaves the river to explore a cove or climb a small ridge. Swimming holes along the broad, slow-moving rivers invite the summer visitor. The forest consists of large hardwood trees and little undergrowth; cypress and oak grow at the river's edge.

In addition to great scenery, Turkey Creek's excellent singletrack serves up some fun technical moves. You'll encounter a dozen wooden bridges, many that require a pop-a-wheelie on the approach. Enjoy tight switchbacks, log jumps, a set of whoop-dee-do's, and several wet crossings.

Unfortunately, the trail is in need of some repair. One bridge was out when I rode Turkey Creek, and the last 2 miles were overgrown in places. Nevertheless, the trail deserves two thumbs up!

Note: Many riders make a loop by following a network of Forest Service roads back to Key Bridge. Contact the Long Cane Ranger District of Sumter National Forest for a map of the area (see Appendix A).

Turkey Creek Trail •
Steven's Creek Trail

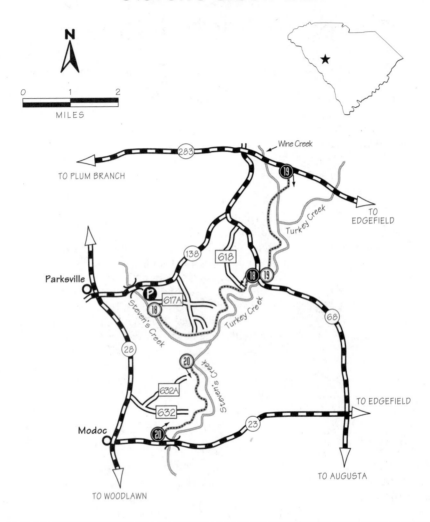

THE RIDE

0.0 Travel down an old roadbed marked with a trail sign.

0.1 Note the old bridge across Turkey Creek to the left as the trail curves to the right and becomes singletrack.

0.7 At a fork, stay left.

0.8 Come out at the end of Forest Road 618 and head left into the woods. Immediately take a right onto singletrack.

2.9 Caution! Sharp switchback with a drop-off to the creek.

4.8 Red trail sign. Turn left to see the confluence of Turkey and Steven's creeks. Turn right to continue the ride, now parallel with Steven's Creek.

5.2 At the junction with an old roadbed, go left onto singletrack.

5.3 Cross a powerline cut.

7.1 Leave the river and ascend through dense pine.

7.5 Arrive at the end of FR 617A.

Turkey Creek Trail (North)

<table>
<tr><td>See Map on Page 66</td><td></td><td></td></tr>
</table>

Location:	About 15 miles southeast of McCormick, north of Key Bridge on Turkey Creek.
Distance:	4.7 miles one way.
Tread:	Singletrack.
Aerobic level:	Easy to moderate; one gradual climb at the end.
Technical difficulty:	3; tight turns, extremely narrow track, steep drop-offs, difficult tributary crossings, limited sight distance, and trail in need of repair.
Land status:	Long Cane Ranger District of Sumter National Forest.
Maps:	USGS Parksville, Clarks Hill; a map is available from the Forest Service.
Access:	Travel south out of McCormick about 4 miles on U.S. Highway 221 to Plum Branch and turn left onto South Carolina 283. Cross SC 138 after 6.7 miles and go another mile to the parking lot on the right. (To set shuttle, park the second vehicle at Key Bridge. Go back to the intersection with SC 138 and turn left. Travel 4 miles and park on the shoulder before the steel bridge.)

HIGHLIGHTS

In contrast to Turkey Trail (South), this singletrack, which follows Turkey Creek north of Key Bridge, has seen better days. This ghost of a trail begins in great condition, but within the first mile it becomes challenging at times to follow the white blazes. Sections are overgrown, briars encroach the path, and high water has moved or mangled many of the dozen footbridges.

The good news? Recently the Forest Service received funds to return the trail to its former glory. Soon you will be able to ride this beautiful riverside trail, which travels through open bottomland and on the slopes of the river's floodplain. Large grapevines line the trail and cypress and oak grow along the riverbank. When the project is complete, you will be able to add this section to Turkey Creek Trail (South) for a total of 12.2 miles of singletrack. Contact Augusta Freewheelers for updates (see Appendix C), or better yet volunteer to help with the improvements.

Kirsten Slusar checks out the map in Sumter National Forest.

0.0 Pass an information board and descend through open pine.

0.8 Cross Wine Creek where you'll see the remains of a beautiful old stone bridge.

2.5 Reach the bluff above Turkey Creek and enjoy excellent views.

2.8 Ride across several wooden bridges in the next 0.1 mile.

3.3 Cross a pipeline cut.

3.8 Ride over four more bridges in the next 0.2 mile.

4.3 Walk your bike through the last ravine, where the bridge lies washed up next to trail.

4.7 Reach the southern trailhead at Key Bridge.

Steven's Creek Trail

See Map on Page 66	
Location:	About 15 miles southeast of McCormick, near Modoc Bridge on Steven's Creek.
Distance:	11 miles out and back.
Tread:	Singletrack.
Aerobic level:	Moderate to difficult; many short climbs.
Technical difficulty:	3; Roots, loose rock, tight turns, steep drop-offs, and a different test at each ravine.
Land status:	Long Cane Ranger District of Sumter National Forest.
Maps:	USGS Parksville, Clarks Hill; a map is available from the Forest Service.
Access:	Travel about 13 miles south out of McCormick on U.S. Highway 221 to Modoc and turn left onto South Carolina 23 (at the BP station). Go 1.2 miles on SC 23 to the parking area on the left before the bridge.

HIGHLIGHTS

Steven's Creek, preferred by many local riders for its technical challenges, is tougher than both Horn Creek and Turkey Creek trails. This out and back offers steeper hills, tight switchbacks, numerous tributary crossings, and abrupt drop-offs to the creek. In places it's smooth sailing on fast singletrack, but then your speed is interrupted by difficult moves at a dozen ravines.

Begin following Steven's Creek upstream through an open forest of upland hardwoods, then border the floodplain and pedal through bottomland.

Negotiating a bridge on the Steven's Creek Trail.

The trail along the bluff above the creek is contrasted by a section of pine forest away from the creek. Several places along the trail access swimming holes on Steven's Creek.

The singletrack beyond mile 5.5, which is marked by a sign posted on a tree, leaves national forest land. In the future, permission may be granted to continue the ride out to the confluence of Turkey and Steven's creeks. Contact the Augusta Freewheelers for updates (see Appendix C).

THE RIDE

0.0 Follow the white-blazed singletrack and cross a wooden bridge.
0.3 Attempt the technical, rocky crossing of Key Branch.
0.5 On an ascent, ride over several rubber tire scraps made into water bars.
2.2 Reach a high bluff above Steven's Creek and enjoy the view.
3.3 Another good view.
4.2 Cross the largest ravine on a long wooden bridge.
5.3 Final view of Steven's Creek.
5.5 Intersection. An old roadbed enters from the left and the trail ahead leaves public land. Turn around and retrace the ride.
11.0 Arrive back at the parking lot.

Horn Creek Trail

Location:	About 25 miles southeast of McCormick in the Lick Fork Recreation Area.
Distance:	5.7-mile loop.
Tread:	Wide singletrack.
Aerobic level:	Moderate; easy riding with a 1-mile gentle climb and one short steep.
Technical difficulty:	2/3; a set of wooden steps, several bridges, and a short rocky section.
Land status:	Long Cane Ranger District of Sumter National Forest.
Maps:	USGS Colliers; a map is available from the Forest Service.
Access:	Travel south out of McCormick on U.S. Highway 221 about 13 miles to Modoc. Turn left onto South Carolina 23 and drive 9 miles to SC 230. Turn right here, drive 0.4 mile, and turn left onto Lick Fork Road (State Route 263). Drive another 1.9 miles, then turn right into the recreation area. After the

Horn Creek Trail

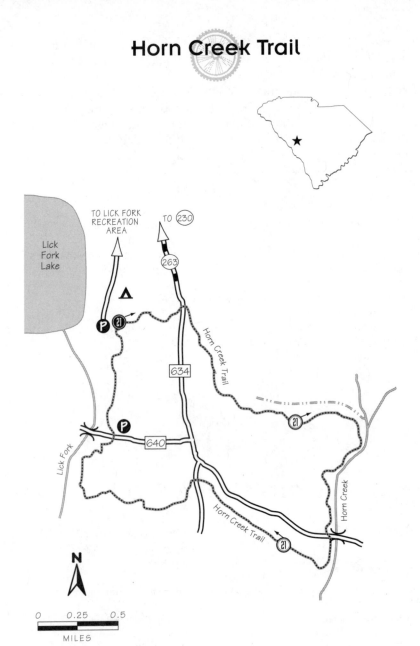

Lick Fork Lake

TO LICK FORK RECREATION AREA

TO 230

263

634

640

Horn Creek Trail

Lick Fork

Horn Creek

Horn Creek Trail

21

N

0   0.25   0.5

MILES

information board (where you must pay a nominal entrance fee), turn left onto the gravel road. Drive 0.5 mile to the parking area at the end of the road. For alternative parking at no charge, continue on Lick Fork Road 0.9 mile past the entrance to the recreation area. (The road becomes gravel Forest Road 634.) Turn right onto FR 640, drive 0.4 mile, and locate the parking lot on the right before the creek. You will be at mile 4.9 of the ride.

HIGHLIGHTS

Many mountain bikers consider Horn Creek Trail the most popular ride in Sumter National Forest. The excellent singletrack is definitely the Forest Service's pride and joy.

The scenery of this rolling Piedmont country is hard to beat. For much of the loop, you will parallel Horn Creek and Lick Fork. In the beautiful bottoms area, you will ride through open hardwood forest and cross a creek on a set of bridges built by a Georgia Eagle Scout troop. The wooded ridge section delivers the sweet smell of pine and a gentle 1-mile climb.

Horn Creek Trail is maintained by the Augusta Freewheelers under the Forest Service Volunteer Program. The trail crew works to keep the loop free of obstacles, making this wide singletrack ideal for introducing someone to the sport. Experts also ride here, traveling this fast loop as many as five times.

Horn Creek Trail is located in the Lick Fork Recreation Area. Enjoy the picnic area and small, wooded campground on the shore of the 12-acre Lick Fork Lake. You will also find a boat ramp, a public swimming area, and a 2-mile nature trail that circles the lake.

THE RIDE

0.0 From the Lick Fork Recreation Area parking lot, head up and to the left, following the sign for Horn Creek to ride the loop clockwise. You will pass a primitive campsite on the left.

0.4 Cross the first of several gravel roads; continue straight.

1.1 Reach a beautiful bottoms area where you will cross a creek on a set of wooden bridges.

2.7 Cross the second gravel road and begin a wooded section of trail.

3.7 Cross a third gravel road.

4.0 A roadbed parallels the trail on the left. You will cross it several times.

4.5 Ride along another creek, following it upstream.

4.9 Turn left onto a gravel road and ride about 75 yards to a small parking lot. Return to the woods on singletrack.

5.5 Trail junction. Take the left fork, toward the creek, then go upstream and cross a wooden bridge.

Tim Malson on the Horn Creek Trail. Jim Schmid Photo

5.6 Pass the sluiceway and dam below Lick Fork Lake and begin a short, steep ascent.

5.7 Reach the parking lot at the recreation area.

Harbison State Forest

Harbison State Forest, primarily developed to teach forest management and the wise use of forest natural resources, offers a 2,200-acre mountain bike playground for Columbia locals and area visitors. The facility is located inside the city limits of South Carolina's capital—a kind of green oasis just 9 miles from downtown.

At the turn of the century, this area was mostly cotton fields, and 20 or so years later, the land yielded timber primarily. After the South Carolina Forestry Commission bought this tract in 1951, the land was allowed to recover. In the 1980s, the commission created a teaching forest.

Bordered to the northeast by the Broad River, Harbison State Forest is filled with loblolly, short-leaf, and long-leaf pine, as well as bottomland hardwoods and hardwood drains. Many of the long-leaf pines are marked with V-cuts made when rosin was collected to be processed and used by the naval industry.

Mountain bikers are the largest user group of Harbison State Forest. The commission publishes a detailed map that corresponds to lettered trail markers. Pick up a map at one of the information boards, which are located at the trailhead parking lots.

Harbison offers excellent singletrack, which is somewhat technical without being difficult. Expect good conditions except after excessive rain. Local hammerheads ride fast and hard here, so be alert—especially during the late afternoon and on weekends.

The facilities at the state forest include a picnic area, a large playing field, a gazebo shelter, and a restroom.

Important note: Biking permits, which are required for all state forests in South Carolina, are available at the Harbison office or through the mail from the South Carolina Forestry Commission. Individual permits are $3, daily, and $15, annually. The forest office is open on weekdays. Be sure to plan ahead if you are not visiting the forest during office hours. For more information, contact Harbison State Forest (see Appendix A).

A beautiful day on superlative South Carolina singletrack. JIM SCHMID PHOTO

Stewardship Trail

Location:	9 miles northwest of Columbia in Harbison State Forest.
Distance:	3-mile loop.
Tread:	Singletrack.
Aerobic level:	Moderate; rolling hills.
Technical difficulty:	3-; wide bridges, tree roots, tight turns, and a fun creek crossing.
Land status:	Harbison State Forest.
Maps:	USGS Irmo, Columbia North; a complete map of the area is available at the information boards in the state forest.
Access:	Traveling on Interstate 26, go 9 miles west of Columbia, take Exit 103 (Harbison Boulevard and turn left at the light. Proceed to Broad River Road, turn right, go through a traffic light, and turn left into Harbison State Forest. After 0.1 mile, veer left through the entrance gate and begin driving on the main gravel road. Travel 2 miles and park on the right in lot number 6.

HIGHLIGHTS

This trail symbolizes the forest's stewardship philosophy—tending to our woodlands with regard to the environment as a whole. The area around the trail is often used to get people involved in the forest's management programs.

The Stewardship Trail is the most technical of the three loops at Harbison. You won't find any difficult moves, but the constant, easy challenges of tight turns and tree roots will demand good riding skills. Too bad this singletrack loop is so short. Locals often ride it twice, once in each direction for a good afternoon pump.

Enjoy the creek crossing, which is optional. A fork in the trail lets you choose a bridge or the water. And don't miss the spur that leads to River Rest, an overlook on the Broad River.

THE RIDE

0.0 Ride past the information board and head into the woods.
0.4 Reach a bench along the trail. You are probably not tired enough to sit down yet!

Stewardship Trail • Midlands Mountain Trail • Firebreak Trail • Harbison Loop

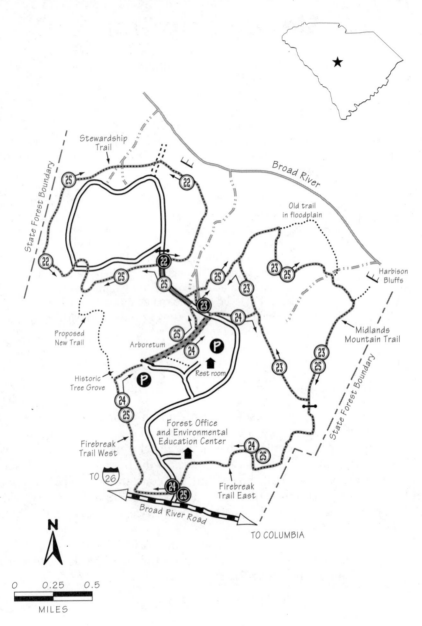

0.7 Look for the marker for River Rest. A 100-yard spur takes you to the banks of the Broad River.

0.9 Cross a grassy road. To the left (0.6 mile), the gravel road; to the right, a field on the Broad River often used by Scout groups.

1.1 At a fork, go left to cross the creek on a bridge and go right for a good creek crossing.

2.1 Cross a gravel road, enter the woods, and cross the road again.

3.0 Reach parking lot number 6.

Midlands Mountain Trail

Location:	9 miles northwest of Columbia in Harbison State Forest.
Distance:	3.6-mile loop.
Tread:	Singletrack.
Aerobic level:	Moderate; one good climb.
Technical difficulty:	2+; one climb rates a 3 because of water bars and switchbacks.
Land status:	Harbison State Forest.
Maps:	USGS Irmo, Columbia North; a complete map of the area is available at the information boards in the state forest.
Access:	Same as Ride 22. From the entrance to the forest, travel 1.6 miles and park on the right in lot number 5.

See Map on Page 78

HIGHLIGHTS

The Midlands Mountain Trail, the oldest loop at Harbison, used to lie in the floodplain of the Broad River, and occasionally, in years past, part of the trail has been inundated. A new section of trail built in 1996 keeps the route on the ridge.

The trail covers a variety of biocommunities. You will pedal through river floodplain, as well as pine woodlands, bottom hardwoods, north slopes, and coves. The floodplain attracts wildlife to this part of the forest. I saw deer and wild turkeys on my ride. Be sure to take the detour to Harbison Bluffs for winter views of the Broad River.

Sandra Schmid cruising through upland forest country. JIM SCHMID PHOTO

0.0 Pass the information board and head into the woods.

0.1 At a T intersection, turn right and ride across a wooden bridge. Then begin the steep, 0.3-mile climb with water bars and switchbacks.

0.4 At a second T intersection, go left to travel the Midlands Mountain Trail clockwise.

1.3 Cross the first of two bridges at the low point of the floodplain.

1.6 A 0.1-mile spur trail leads to Harbison Bluffs.

2.3 Trail junction with Firebreak Trail East. Turn right to continue the loop.

3.2 Arrive back at the second T intersection and turn left to retrace the first 0.4 mile of your ride.

3.5 Be sure to turn left after the wooden bridge to return to your car.

3.6 Reach parking lot number 5.

Firebreak Trail

See Map on Page 78	

Location: 9 miles northwest of Columbia in Harbison State Forest.

Distance: 4.3-mile loop.

Tread: Singletrack.

Aerobic level: Moderate; rolling hills.

Technical difficulty: 2; some tight turns and tree roots.

Land status: Harbison State Forest.

Maps: USGS Irmo, Columbia North; a complete map of the area is available at the information boards in the state forest.

Access: Same as Ride 22 to the Harbison State Forest. After turning off of Broad River Road, park immediately on your left at the information board (lot number 1).

HIGHLIGHTS

A portion of the Midlands Mountain Trail connects Firebreak Trail West and Firebreak Trail East to create the longest designated loop in the forest. Locals consider the West an entrance trail and the East an exit trail from the forest.

The trail runs through Harbison's Arboretum, a 260-acre area designated for the identification and study of native trees and those suitable to the state's urban environment. The trail also passes the Historic Tree Grove, which was initially started by ladie's clubs several years ago. Seeds and cuttings bought through the American Forestry Association are planted here for visitors to appreciate. The grove showcases historic trees like the angel oak from Charleston.

THE RIDE

0.0 Ride to the back of the parking lot to locate the trailhead of Firebreak West.

1.0 Ride past the Historic Tree Grove.

1.2 Go straight through parking lot number 4 and around the gate. Begin riding on an old roadbed.

1.3 A detour to the right leads to the restrooms; otherwise, continue straight. You will pass fields that are part of the arboretum.

1.5 At a fork, head right down a wide, rocky section of trail.

1.7 Cross the main gravel road.

2.0 At a T intersection, turn right and begin riding on a wider section of trail.

2.6 Turn right and ride around a gate to pick up Firebreak East.

3.1 Pass a water tower.

3.9 Cross a seeded roadbed.

4.1 Cross the gravel road that leads to the forest headquarters.

4.2 Cross the main gravel road again.

4.3 Reach parking lot number 1.

Harbison Loop

See Map
on Page 78

Location:	9 miles northwest of Columbia in Harbison State Forest.
Distance:	9.3-mile loop.
Tread:	Singletrack with 0.8 mile on gravel road.
Aerobic level:	Moderate; rolling hills with one good climb.
Technical difficulty:	3; tight turns, tree roots, wide bridges, a creek crossing, and a steep ascent with water bars and switchbacks.
Land status:	Harbison State Forest.
Maps:	USGS Irmo, Columbia North; a complete map of the area is available at the information boards in the state forest.
Access:	Same as Ride 24.

Jack Martin wisely dismounts before crossing a narrow bridge. JIM SCHMID PHOTO

HIGHLIGHTS

Combine the forest's three loops and you have the locals' favorite ride. Use Firebreak West as an entrance trail and the Firebreak East as an exit trail for this loop. You can ride the main gravel road to connect with the Stewardship Trail, or use the recently completed 1.5-mile link, which eliminates the gravel. Contact Cycle Center for more information (see Appendix B).

THE RIDE

0.0 Ride to the back of the parking lot to locate the trailhead for Firebreak West.

1.2 Go through parking lot number 4 and around the gate. Begin riding on an old roadbed.

1.3 A detour to the right leads to the restrooms; otherwise, continue straight.

1.5 Take a left at a fork.

1.7 Turn left and begin riding on the main gravel road.

2.1 Reach the Stewardship Trail and turn left, riding the loop clockwise.

3.0 Cross a gravel road and ride into woods, then cross the road again.

4.2 Cross a grassy road.

4.5 Turn left if you want to visit River Rest.

5.1 Arrive at parking lot number 6 and turn left onto the main gravel road again.

5.5 Turn left onto singletrack, 0.1 mile before parking lot number 5. After crossing a wooden bridge, begin a 0.3-mile steep ascent with water bars and switchbacks.

5.8 At the T intersection, go left to ride Midlands Mountains Trail clockwise.

5.9 Cross a pair of bridges, the low point of the floodplain.

7.0 A 0.1-mile spur trail leads to Harbison Bluffs.

7.7 Turn left and ride around a gate to pick up Firebreak East.

8.9 Cross a seeded roadbed.

9.1 Cross the gravel road that leads to the forest headquarters.

9.2 Cross the main gravel road.

9.3 Arrive back at parking lot number 1.

Sesquicentennial State Park

During the celebration of Columbia's 150th anniversary, the Sesquicentennial commission sold souvenir coins and used the proceeds to buy the private holdings that now comprise Sesquicentennial State Park. Opened in June 1940, the park was dedicated to the recreation of the people, and it lives up to this objective. In addition to the popular singletrack mountain bike loop, the park serves Columbia with a jogging track, nature trails, lake swimming, a picnic area, and an excellent campground.

Generally referred to as "Sesqui," this 1,419-acre park lies in the Sandhills region of the state, where sand was deposited by an ancient sea. You will pedal through pine and scrub oak forest where once there were sand dunes.

Sesqui's historic Log House, located near the trailhead, was built in 1756 and demonstrates the construction style of German pioneers. Considered the oldest home in Richland County, the building serves as a studio and gallery for resident artist Campbell Frost, who teaches classes to the public several days a week.

There is a $2 parking fee per vehicle on weekends from Easter to mid-October, and on weekdays from Memorial Day to Labor Day. Contact Sesquicentennial State Park for more information (see Appendix A).

Sesqui Mountain Bike Trail

Location:	13 miles northeast of Columbia in Sesquicentennial State Park.
Distance:	6.1-mile loop.
Tread:	Sandy singletrack with 2 miles on a hard-packed sandy road.
Aerobic level:	Moderate; short ups and downs.
Technical difficulty:	2+; some patches of soft sand, a few tight turns, lots of tree roots, and one creek crossing on boardwalk.
Land status:	Sesquicentennial State Park.
Maps:	USGS Fort Jackson North; a map is available from the park office.
Access:	Traveling east on Interstate 20 toward Florence, take Exit 74 and turn left onto U.S. Highway 1 (Two Notch Road). Go 3 miles, turn right into Sesqui State Park, and drive another 0.7 mile to the sand parking lot on the left.

Sesqui Mountain Bike Trail

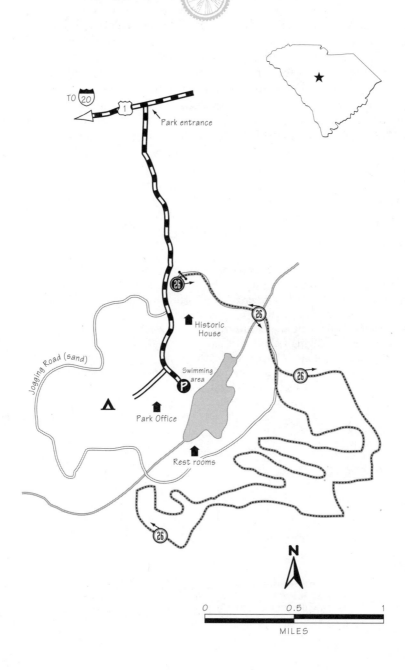

HIGHLIGHTS

The Sesqui Mountain Bike Trail's proximity to Columbia and accessibility from three major interstates adds to its popularity. The sandy singletrack was built on a terraced area of the park, and you can ride fast on this gentle roller coaster without fear of encountering many technical difficulties.

The loop has been used for races to raise money for the American Lung Association, and Cycle Center has sponsored a few small events. Due to the sandy tread, Sesqui is better after heavy rain than the neighboring Harbison State Forest. I had a good ride early one morning after a downpour.

The trail starts at the park's fitness circuit, so begin your workout with a few pull-ups or dips on the apparatus. Finish off your ride with a swim in the lake, located 0.3 mile from the trailhead at the end of the park road.

THE RIDE

0.0 Pass an information board and ride through a fitness area to locate the trailhead. The blue-blazed trail begins as a hard-packed sandy road.

0.9 Disregard the 1-mile marker for the jogging trail and follow the blue arrows. Take a left at a fork onto an old roadbed.

1.0 Reach a trail junction and turn right onto singletrack.

1.8 Pass a large playing field on the left.

2.6 Ride across a 30-foot boardwalk.

3.0 Access trail to restrooms, water, and picnic shelters. Scramble down through the woods and cross the sand jogging road.

3.2 Enjoy several ascending switchbacks.

5.0 After a short, steep descent with a tight turn, reach the sand jogging road and turn right.

6.1 Arrive back at your vehicle.

Jim Schmid, state trails coordinator, trying to establish contact with extraterrestrials in the Sesquicentennial State Forest. JIM SCHMID PHOTO

Sand Hills State Forest

Visit Sand Hills State Forest to ride one of South Carolina's newest mountain bike trails. Local rider Mike Ratterree, along with several other volunteers, constructed the trail, and word of their superb effort is traveling fast.

The 46,000-acre Sand Hills State Forest, which extends from Lynches River up to Cheraw State Park, is primarily managed for timber. The forest, which is adjacent to Sand Hills Wildlife Refuge, is dominated by long-leaf pine, but you will also find small stands of other pine species, as well as hickories, red and white oaks, and yellow poplars. With prescribed burning and thinning, the forestry commission assists in the management of the endangered red-cockaded woodpecker, a small black-and-white bird that makes its nest in old-growth timber.

Biking permits, which are required for all state forests in South Carolina, are available at the Sand Hills office or through the mail from the South Carolina Forestry Commission. Individual permits are $3 daily, and $15, annually. Be sure to plan ahead if you are not visiting the forest during office hours.

Facilities at the trailhead are limited. You will find an information board, picnic tables, and a mailbox for registering. You will need a permit (no charge) to camp at one of the forest's eight primitive sites. Note: Hunting is allowed in the forest, and deer season usually runs the month of October. Be sure to check at the forest office for regulations and specific dates. For more information, contact Sand Hills State Forest (see Appendix A).

Sand Hills Mountain Bike Trail

Location:	45 miles northwest of Florence in the Sand Hills State Forest.
Distance:	8-mile loop.
Tread:	Singletrack.
Aerobic level:	Moderate; a few good climbs.
Technical difficulty:	3; tight turns, roots, and log jumps.
Land status:	Sand Hills State Forest.
Maps:	USGS Patrick, Middendorf; a map is available from the state forest.
Access:	Travel 10 miles north of McBee on U.S. Highway 1 and look on the left for the sign marking the headquarters of Sand Hills State Forest. Turn right on a sandy road and drive 0.3 mile to the small parking area on the right.

Sand Hill Mountain Bike Trail

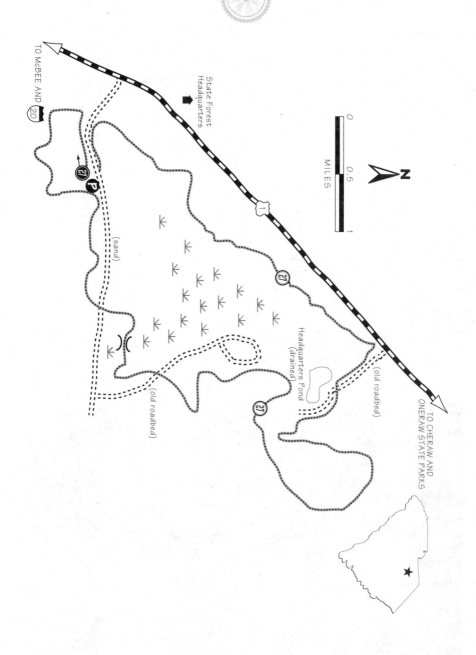

TO McBEE AND (20)

State Forest Headquarters

(sand)

P

27

27

(old roadbed)

(old roadbed)

Headquarters Pond (drained)

27

TO CHERAW AND ONERAW STATE PARKS

MILES
0   0.5   1

N

89

HIGHLIGHTS

On this tight, sandy singletrack, you will constantly rub elbows with pine trees. The challenges of this action-packed loop include 90-degree turns, difficult log crossings, and a new 40-foot bridge over the creek. Be ready for several slow-speed, technical areas, as well as a section of roller-coaster hills. Plans include extending the loop west across U.S. Highway 1 for 20 miles of continuous trail.

THE RIDE

0.0 Head out on the trail beyond a mailbox. Please be sure to register and feel free to make comments.

0.8 Trail travels through a clearcut.

1.3 An open section near the top of a hill offers a nice view to the left.

1.6 Cross a sandy Forest Service road.

2.0 A new 40-foot bridge crosses the creek.

2.3 Cross an old roadbed and climb gradually.

3.0 Begin the roller-coaster section—fun hills with a decent climb at the end.

3.3 Another good view to the left at the top of a hill.

3.5 Follow an "extension" sign right.

3.7 Cross another old roadbed.

4.1 Begin the first of two short switchback climbs.

A trailhead in the Sand Hills State Forest. JIM SCHMID PHOTO

4.4 At a fork, follow the trail to the left (the right fork leads onto a proprosed extension of the trail).

5.0 An arrow points left. Follow the singletrack as it widens to a rutted old roadbed and travels right.

5.3 Merge with a dirt road after passing a drained pond. Continue left.

5.6 Reach U.S. Highway 1 and parallel the road for a while. Soon the trail cuts left into the woods.

7.8 Enter an open field and continue to the sandy Forest Service road, which you took to reach the trailhead parking. Turn left.

8.0 Arrive back at your vehicle.

Manchester State Forest

Now a town of the past, Manchester was a main depot along the Old King's Highway between Camden and Charleston in the early 1800s. Later in the century, plantation owners settled along the Wateree River. During the Depression, the federal government began buying up depleted land, and in 1956, title was given to the state for the purpose of developing a state forest. Manchester State Forest is composed of three former estates and now totals over 23,000 acres.

Located between the Sandhills region of the state and the coastal plain, Manchester consists of a mix from both areas—ridges and sandhills, and swamps and hardwood bottoms. With 65 percent of the forest's base destroyed by Hurricane Hugo in 1989, the forestry commission has been busy replanting. Recently, Manchester has seen an increase in recreational use with equestrians, hikers, motorcycles, and mountain bikers sharing this unique forest.

Poinsett State Park, located about 0.5 mile past the trailhead on Park Road, provides year-round camping and rustic rental cabins. In the summer, visit the lake for a post-ride swim. The park also offers a picnic area and nature center.

In general, the hunting season for large game occurs from October through December, and bikers may ride in the forest on Sundays only. Small game season runs through February, and bikers may ride any time at their own risk. Be sure to check at the forest office for specific dates, which are set in July.

Biking permits, which are required for all state forests in South Carolina, are available at the Manchester office or through the mail from the South Carolina Forestry Commission. Individual permits are $3, daily, and $15, annually. The forest office is open on weekdays. Be sure to plan ahead if you are not visiting the forest during office hours. For more information, contact the Manchester State Forest (see Appendix A).

Killer Three Loop

Location:	20 miles southwest of Sumter in the Manchester State Forest.
Distance:	7.5-mile loop.
Tread:	Singletrack with 0.2 mile on pavement and 0.5 mile on gravel road.
Aerobic level:	Moderate; the last mile adds a strenuous leg.
Technical difficulty:	3-; several logs, some soft sand, and a few tight turns.

Killer Three Loop

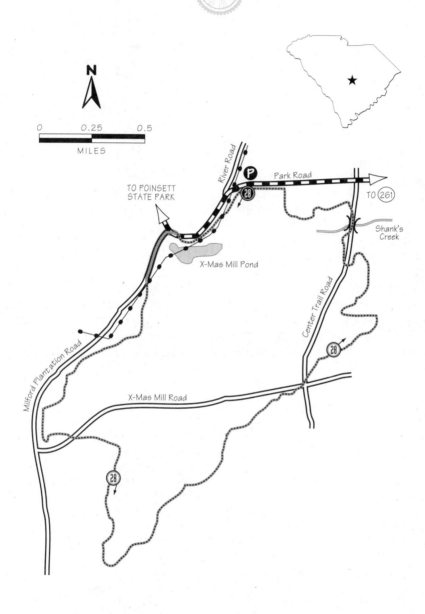

N

0   0.25   0.5
MILES

TO POINSETT
STATE PARK

River Road

Park Road

P

28

TO 261

Shank's
Creek

X-Mas Mill Pond

Center Trail Road

28

Milford Plantation Road

X-Mas Mill Road

28

Land status: Manchester State Forest.

Maps: USGS Poinsett State Park; a map is available from the state forest.

Access: From Interstate 95 near Manning, take Exit 119 and follow South Carolina 261 (for about 18 miles) through Paxville and Pinewood. Turn left onto Park Road (State Route 63) and travel 1.2 miles to a gravel parking lot on the left before the junction of River Road.

HIGHLIGHTS

Mountain bikers have been racing in Manchester State Forest for ten years. After Hurricane Hugo in 1989, the current loop was built and is maintained by the Sumter Chain Gang Cycling Club (see Appendix C). The club, along with Buddy's Schwinn Cycling and Fitness, sponsors a series of races—the Killer Three—during the first three months of every year. For more information, contact Buddy's Schwinn Cycling and Fitness (see Appendix B).

The hilly terrain of the Killer Three Loop, seemingly out of place for this part of the state, creates a gentle, rolling ride. While Manchester is not quite a climber's trail, the semitight singletrack is fairly technical with some sharp diagonal turns that will challenge the novice rider. Several straightaways deliver a string of whoop-dee-do's, produced by motorcyclists that used to ride through the trail as part of the Sumter County Enduro Race.

THE RIDE:

0.0 Ride the trail out of the parking area parallel to the paved road and follow the trail along the powerline for 0.2 mile. The trail markers are blue signs with the bicycle emblem.

0.3 At X-mas Mill Pond, take a sharp right turn, ascend to the pavement, and turn left.

0.5 Turn left onto the sandy Milford Plantation Road, before the entrance to Poinsett State Park, and begin a gentle climb.

0.8 Follow the singletrack left into the woods.

2.2 Cross the gravel X-mas Mill Road.

3.1 Reach a confusing junction. Head left down a short steep.

4.6 Come out of the woods at the junction of Center Trail and X-mas Mill Road. Cross diagonally and re-enter the woods.

5.1 Pass through an open field.

5.8 At the top of a short climb, go left.

5.9 Cross the dirt Center Trail Road.

6.1 Reach Center Trail Road again and follow it left.

6.2 Cross over Shank's Creek.

6.3 Turn left into the woods on singletrack and begin the hardest mile of the ride.

7.3 Reach the paved Park Road, turn right, and ride along the shoulder.

7.5 Return to the parking area.

Enjoying the wooded singletrack in South Carolina.

Santee State Park

Located on the banks of Lake Marion, Santee is one of the most popular parks in the state. Anglers make up 80 percent of the visitors because this 2,500-acre vacation spot is known nationwide for bass fishing.

While Santee is not a mountain biker's destination, the park intends to improve the entire trail system. By the summer of 1998 you can expect about 7 miles of new trail in the triangle between State Park Road and Cleveland Road. The plans include a route closer to the lake, a large loop off the main out-and-back trail, and several connector trails linked to the pavement to create shorter loops.

In addition to fishing and bike trails, the park offers lakeshore campsites and unusual cabins built on piers extending into the water. The Lakeview Restaurant serves southern cooking, and the Interpretive Center provides information about the history of Lake Marion, which was a hydroelectric and navigational project of the late 1930s. There is also a store and a picnic area. For more information, contact Santee State Park (see Appendix A).

Lakeshore Trail

Location:	25 miles east of Orangeburg in Santee State Park, on the south shore of Lake Marion.
Distance:	7 miles out and back.
Tread:	Wide old roadbed.
Aerobic level:	Easy.
Technical difficulty:	1; only a few rocks and debris.
Land status:	Santee State Park.
Maps:	USGS Summerton, Vance; a map is available from the state park.
Access:	Traveling southwest from Manning on Interstate 95, cross Lake Marion and take Exit 98. Follow South Carolina 6 west through Santee for 1 mile; turn right onto State Park Road and travel 2.2 miles to a stop sign. Cross Cleveland Road and continue straight for 1.8 miles to a small dirt parking lot on the right.

Lakeshore Trail

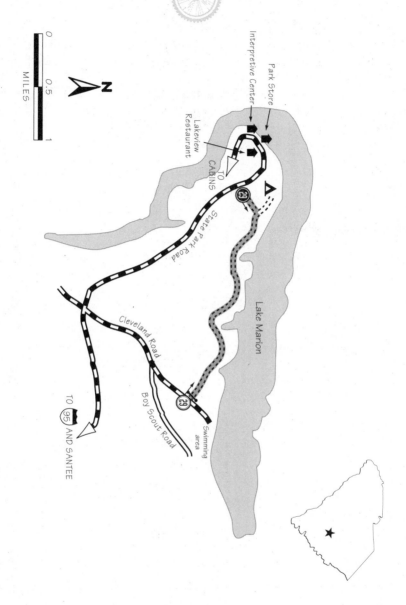

HIGHLIGHTS

Until the new singletrack is complete, the Lakeshore Trail offers a pleasant ride. This shaded old roadbed consists of grass and hard-packed sand and runs parallel to Lake Marion, with occasional views of the water. The trail ends near the swimming area.

On the Lakeshore Trail, which extends half the length of the park, you will pedal through a pine-hardwood forest with an understory of dogwood and sassafras. Several live oaks line the lakeshore. Take a ride at dusk and you are sure to see wild turkey and deer.

THE RIDE

0.0 Head into the woods on an old roadbed.

0.3 At a junction, turn right to ride the bike trail.

3.5 Reach a gate at Cleveland Road. Turn around and retrace your path to the parking lot. Or, head left on the pavement to the swimming area.

The Lowcountry

The coast of South Carolina stretches for almost 200 miles from the Little River near the North Carolina border to the southern tip of Hilton Head Island. When you add all the islands, peninsulas, and bays, the total shoreline comes to about 3,000 miles. This is a land of mysterious swamps, saltwater marshes, tidal creeks, fertile plantations, and South Carolina's state tree—the palmetto.

Two-hundred-year-old homes stand as reminders of a grand way of life—quiet wealth and polished charm. Live oaks draped in Spanish moss line many of the back roads. Historic rice fields echo a time between the 1700s and 1900s when the Old South prospered, largely because of this crop. The coast of South Carolina was once the most productive rice-growing area in the United States.

The Lowcountry is popular as a year-round vacation destination and a choice retirement spot. The northern section of the coastline consists of a strip of wide, white sand known as the Grand Strand, some of the loveliest beaches on the southern U.S. coast. Myrtle Beach is the king of the booming resort areas on this 60-mile stretch. You can enjoy luxurious golf courses, deep-sea fishing, oceanside boardwalks, and dinner cruises.

Farther south, beginning in Georgetown, the shoreline becomes more irregular, broken by peninsulas and inlets. Semitropical islands dot the coastline and invite you to enjoy the solitude of windswept beaches, vast salt marshes, and blackwater rivers. The remote islands, with a history of pirates and blockade runners, are now resorts. Beachcombing is a popular activity, as well as the general lounging that seems to come with coastal breezes and the sound of the sea. Two of the rides in this book are on Lowcountry sea islands—Edisto Island and Hunting Island.

Sea island culture still exists throughout much of the Lowcountry. Examples include the woven sweetgrass baskets sold at roadside stands and the musical language still spoken by some of the African Americans.

In contrast, Hilton Head, one of the largest sea islands along the South Carolina coast, boasts luxurious accommodations, huge plantations, and championship golf courses. This popular vacation area is worth a visit after a ride at Pinckney National Wildlife Refuge.

Charleston, the heart and soul of South Carolina, is one of the greatest cities in the South and repeatedly rated with the best metropolitan areas as a travel destination. Parts of the city remain much the same as when it was founded in 1670. This historic port epitomizes the Old South in all its genteel elegance and refinement. Charleston's rich heritage is well preserved in many historic churches and buildings—more than 70 pre-Revolutionary structures are still standing.

Spend some time in Charleston and enjoy its cultural vibrancy. Highlights include cobblestone streets, horse-drawn carriage tours, fine museums, beautiful old homes, formal gardens, and wonderful restaurants. After exploring the historic district and the three-block-long Old City Market, head for the beach at Beachwalker Park on the west end of Kiawah Island or Folly Beach County Park on Folly Beach.

Northeast of Charleston, Francis Marion National Forest spreads inland to the shores of Lake Moultrie. There are forests of towering pines, most common of which are loblolly, short-leaf, and slash. To learn more about the forest and its flora and fauna, stop in at Sewee Environmental Center on U.S. Highway 17 in Awendaw, north of Charleston.

The riding in the Lowcountry offers some of the best wildlife viewing in South Carolina. The superb wildlife preserves provide a nesting ground for thousands of waterfowl and migratory birds. Ride in the early morning or late afternoon, and be attentive to wildlife clearings and watering holes. Winter is the best season for bird watching. Look for herons, egrets, sandpipers, ibises, gulls, and pelicans.

American alligators roam in many of the preserves and state parks in the Lowcountry. One such creature gave me quite a scare on my ride at Santee Coastal Reserve. You are most likely to see these large reptiles sunning themselves between March and October.

A variety of lodging options exist in the Lowcountry. Choose from oceanfront or forested tent sites at several state parks, rustic beach cottages on many of the sea islands, and quaint bed-and-breakfasts or elegant hotels in the larger cities. The coast is blessed with many warm winter days, the best time for mountain biking in the Lowcountry, and off-season rates are a bonus.

For information about visiting the coast of South Carolina, contact Charleston Area Convention and Visitors Bureau at 800-868-8118 and the Lowcountry/Resort Islands Tourism Commission at 800-528-6870. Welcome centers are located as you enter the state from Savannah, Georgia, on Interstate 95 and from North Carolina on U.S. Highway 17.

Lake Moultrie

Two freshwater lakes—Lake Moultrie and Lake Marion—were formed in the late 1930s when the Santee and Cooper rivers were dammed for inland navigation and hydroelectric power. The project, endorsed by Franklin Delano Roosevelt, became the largest earth-moving endeavor in the history of the United States. Lake Moultrie covers 60,000 acres and stretches 14 miles across at its widest point.

A 27-mile trail along the northern shore of Lake Moultrie was completed in January 1995 as the first section of the cross-state Palmetto Trail, which will eventually run from the Lowcountry along the Atlantic coast to the foothills of the Blue Ridge Mountains. The majority of the Lake Moultrie Passage follows Santee-Cooper's dike system. (A dike is a raised berm of earth holding back the waters of a lake.) For more information, contact Santee Cooper Land Division, the state-owned electric and water utility company that manages the area (see Appendix A).

Lake Moultrie Passage

Location:	About 60 miles northwest of Charleston, along the north shore of Lake Moultrie.
Distance	26.9 miles one way, plus an additional 6.2 miles out and back at the Sandy Beach area.
Tread:	18.3 miles on dike, 5.1 miles on an old roadbed, 2.8 miles on pavement, and 0.7 mile on singletrack.
Aerobic level:	Easy; although endurance is needed.
Technical difficulty:	1; the short section of boardwalk and singletrack rates a 2.
Land status:	Santee Cooper Land Division.
Maps:	USGS Chicora, Pineville, St. Stephen, Bonneau; a map is available from Palmetto Trails or at the trailhead.
Access:	To reach the trailhead at the Canal Recreation Area, travel north through Charleston on Interstate 26. Take Exit 208 off I-26 and follow U.S. Highway 52 north through Moncks Corner. After US 17A forks off to the right, drive another 3.6 miles on US 52 to the parking area on the left. To reach the trailhead at the Diversion Canal, continue north on US 52 into Saint Stephen and pick up South Carolina 45 west to Pineville. About 6 miles past Pineville, turn left onto Eadie Lane, before the Diversion Canal. The parking lot is 0.8 mile on the right.

HIGHLIGHTS

This long trail incorporates Santee-Cooper's dike system to provide a flat ride around the northern half of Lake Moultrie. You will be rewarded with views across the lake when you reach the top of East Pinopolis Dike, the most scenic portion of the ride. The primitive campsites along this passage make it possible to plan an overnight trip.

Two-thirds of the way into the ride, you'll pass the entrance to the Sandy Beach area. Explore an additional 6.2 miles of trail here. An eagle's nest, lake vistas, and a primitive campsite on the water are among the highlights. Closed from March 2 to November 15, the Sandy Beach area is managed as a quality habitat for waterfowl.

When the dike ends, you will ride on a short railroad trestle across the historic Santee Canal, then you'll encounter an unexpected mile of fun singletrack and an unusual section with boardwalks and a steep arched bridge across Quattlebaum Canal.

Lake Moultrie Passage

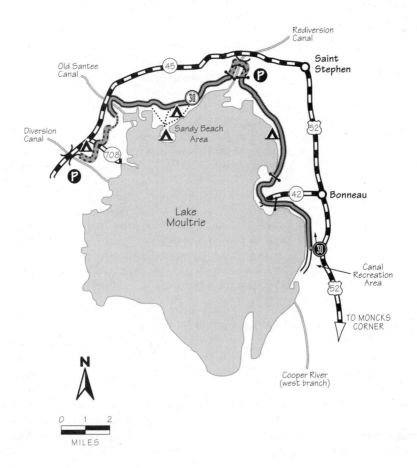

Ben Jones near Lake Moultrie Point. JIM SCHMID PHOTO

THE RIDE

0.0 Cross the canal on a wooden bridge and begin riding on an old grassy road.

0.3 Cross railroad tracks and carry your bike up steep wooden steps to access Pinopolis East Dike. Enjoy views across Lake Moultrie.

4.1 Dike ends at a red gate. Turn left onto paved County Road 42.

4.4 Turn right onto Butter Road.

5.8 Veer right, the paved road changes names to General Moultrie Road.

6.5 Ride straight ahead onto a sandy road and then around a red gate to access the dike again.

8.5 Access to a primitive campsite on the left at double red gates.

12.5 Cross a paved road at Russellville Boat Landing, travel around a red gate, and begin riding on a gravel road that parallels the Rediversion Canal. Note: After 0.3 mile, a railroad trestle crosses the canal, omitting 2 miles of the ride, but authorization has not been obtained to allow trail users to cross here.

17.4 First sign for the Sandy Beach area. Access two primitive campsites and 6.2 miles of additional bike trail.

18.3 Another access to the Sandy Beach area.

21.0 Cross railroad tracks, turn left, and ride the railroad trestle across the historic Santee Canal. Then take a left, ride around a gray gate, and follow an old roadbed for 0.4 mile along the canal.

21.6 At the junction, turn right and continue on a dirt road.

22.0 Begin the boardwalk stretch of the ride.

22.3 Pass a trailer park.

22.6 Cross Quattlebaum Canal on an unusual arched bridge and begin singletrack.

23.3 Singletrack ends. Follow the old roadbed over a bridge, cross the railroad tracks, and begin riding on a sandy road.

24.6 Turn right onto paved Berkeley County Road 708.

25.0 Turn left into the woods and ride around a yellow gate.

25.3 Pass a primitive campsite adjacent to the trail.

26.0 Come out of the woods and bear right on a sandy road.

26.1 Pass a reservoir and follow the powerline cut to the right along Diversion Canal.

26.3 Veer right and ascend.

26.5 Ride around a gray gate.

26.9 Reach the western trailhead.

Santee Coastal Reserve

The Santee Coastal Reserve is primarily a waterfowl management area, but this 24,000-acre sanctuary also supports a variety of other resources and recreation. Adjoining Francis Marion National Forest and Cape Romain National Wildlife Refuge, the reserve lies partly on a delta between two branches of the Santee River and includes several islands. You will find just about every type of coastal environment here: salt marshes, sand dunes, maritime forests, pine flats, cypress swamps, savannahs, mudflats, beach, and Carolina bays. The Santee Indians lived in the region before the arrival of the French Huguenots in the late 1660s. During the 1700s and early 1800s, the area supported a successful plantation of rice and sea island cotton. The Santee Gun Club, a conservation-minded hunting organization formed in 1898, used the land for sport until 1974, when they donated the property to The Nature Conservancy, who later turned it over to the state. Santee is now managed by the South Carolina Department of Natural Resources.

Santee is closed from November through January. On Sundays, the reserve doesn't open until 1 P.M. Phone ahead for other closures. Facilities are limited, and primitive camping requires a free written permit from the reserve office. For more information, contact Santee Coastal Reserve (see Appendix A).

Bike/Hike Trail

Location:	About 22 miles south of Georgetown.
Distance	7.4-mile loop.
Tread:	Old roadbed and dike.
Aerobic level:	Easy.
Technical difficulty:	1; some sections of soft sand, tall grass, roots, and deadfall.
Land status:	South Carolina Department of Natural Resources.
Maps:	USGS Santee, Minim Island, Cape Romain; a map is available from the coastal reserve office.
Access:	At the flashing light in McClellanville, the junction of U.S Highway 17 and South Carolina 45, travel north on US 17 for 6.3 miles to a paved crossroads at an old barn. Turn right on South Santee Road and go 1.5 miles. Turn left between a church and a school onto a dirt road. This is Entrance Avenue, which takes you into the reserve. Drive 2.7 miles and park near the ˋ

Bike/Hike Trail • Marshland Nature Trail

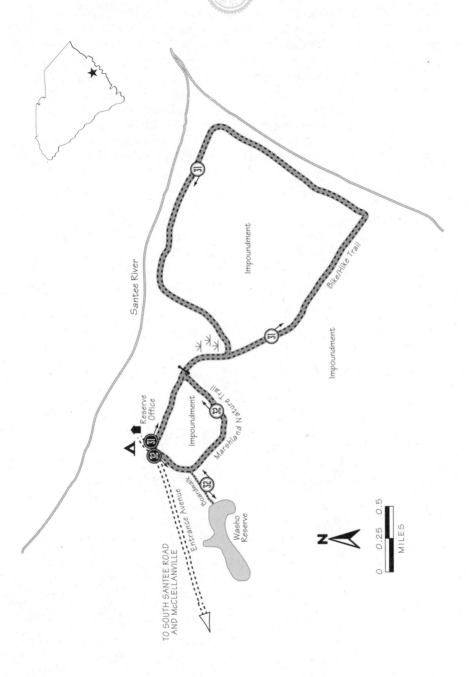

Santee River

Impoundment

Impoundment

Bike/Hike Trail

31

31

Impoundment

32

Marshland Nature Trail

Reserve Office

31

32

Impoundment

32

Boardwalk

Entrance Avenue

Washo Reserve

TO SOUTH SANTEE ROAD AND McCLELLANVILLE

N

0 0.25 0.5
MILES

Cruising through the Santee Coastal Reserve. JIM SCHMID PHOTO

gate and the information board. Note: To reach the reserve office, which is housed in a trailer, fork to the left after the gate.

HIGHLIGHTS

On the Bike/Hike Trail, you'll explore a range of habitats as you parallel the Atlantic Intracoastal Waterway and loop around on a dike system. The impounded waters provide a valuable food source for wildlife and a haven for waterfowl. You can find nearly every species of Atlantic shorebird here. Also keep your eyes peeled for foxes, deer, bobcats, and feral hogs. I saw two alligators on my October ride.

THE RIDE

0.0 Continue straight down the sandy Entrance Avenue on your bike and pass the ranger residence on your left.

0.5 Ride through the maintenance area, then past a small observation boardwalk on the right.

0.7 Go around a gate and begin the Bike/Hike Trail.

1.0 Keep straight; the trail on the left is the other end of the loop.

2.7 Curve around to the left at the trail sign.

6.4 Finish the loop around the impoundment and turn right.

6.7 Return to the gate and continue straight ahead on the sandy road.

7.4 Return to the parking area.

Marshland Nature Trail

Location:	About 22 miles south of Georgetown.
Distance:	1.9-mile loop.
Tread:	Old roadbed.
Aerobic level:	Easy.
Technical difficulty:	1; some sections of soft sand, tall grass, roots, and deadfall.
Land status:	South Carolina Department of Natural Resources.
Maps:	USGS Santee, Minim Island, Cape Romain.
Access:	Same as Ride 31.

See Map on Page 106

HIGHLIGHTS

The Marshland Nature Trail travels around an old rice field and accesses the Marshland boardwalk. You must walk your bike on the boardwalk, but it is worth the stroll to see Washo Reserve, a freshwater cypress lake that provides substantial breeding habitat for osprey. Consider adding this loop to the Bike/Hike Trail. It passes the gate that leads out to the dike system at mile 1.3.

THE RIDE

0.0 Ride behind the information board and across the grass to pick up the Marshland Nature Trail at the edge of the woods.

0.1 Reach the Washo Boardwalk on the right.

0.2 At a sandy road, turn right.

0.3 Take the grassy road on the left.

0.5 Ride along a small impoundment.

0.8 At a Y intersection, go left on the sandy road.

1.3 Turn left to finish the loop and return to your vehicle. (Or turn right, ride around the gate, and begin the Bike/Hike Trail.)

1.5 Pass a small observation boardwalk on the left, then ride through the maintenance area.

1.7 Begin riding on the sandy Entrance Avenue.

1.9 Return to the information board.

A marshland boardwalk in the Santee Coastal Reserve.

Francis Marion National Forest

The 250,000-acre Francis Marion National Forest, located along the coast of South Carolina, was named for a well-known Revolutionary War hero, Francis Marion. Marion's tactics against the British earned him the nickname Swamp Fox. He was famous for attacking the enemy and then disappearing into the dense swamp like a fox to hide safely with his troops.

Lumber companies bought the land after the Civil War and then sold it to the government in the 1930s, when it was declared a national forest. Francis Marion covers much of the coast between the Santee River and Charleston, and extends inland to Lake Moultrie. The forest is divided into two districts—Wambaw and Witherbee.

You will find a variety of ecosystems in Francis Marion. This huge, undeveloped tract of land includes Carolina bays, marshland, swamp, and hardwood bottoms. The pine forests are predominantly loblolly, but you will also see long-leaf pine. Three-fourths of the mature timber was destroyed in 1989 by Hurricane Hugo, and the damage is still evident.

Your visit to the area should include a stop at the Sewee Visitor and Environmental Education Center for displays on the forest's various habitats and an orientation film to the area. Take a short walk to see the live red wolf exhibit. This new facility, 6 miles south of the Swamp Fox Trailhead, provides an opportunity to learn about the valuable ecosystems of the Lowcountry. The staff will be happy to provide recreational information as well.

Buck Hall Recreation Area, along the Intracoastal Waterway, serves Francis Marion National Forest year-round with camping and day-use facilities. This old plantation site has 300 yards of sea wall. Buck Hall is located about 30 miles north of Charleston off U.S. Highway 17; turn right on Forest Road 242. There is also a beautiful picnic area near Huger.

Note: Always check for the presence of hunters when biking in national forests. Before hitting the trail, familiarize yourself with the exact dates of each hunting season, which change each year. For more information, contact the Wambaw or Witherbee Ranger District of Francis Marion National Forest (see Appendix A).

Bonus trail: The Wambaw Cycle Trail offers two loops that create a figure eight, totaling about 40 miles. This is probably one of the longest trail-riding opportunities in the state. The trail is located in the national forest at the Round Pond Cycle Trailhead off Halfway Creek Road. While primarily an ATV/motorcycle trail, Wambaw's old logging roads and sandy singletrack make great riding for the coastal mountain biker. Family Riders Motorcycle Club of Charleston, who has maintained the trail for 20 years, welcomes mountain bike use. For more information, contact the Family Riders Motorcycle Club (see Appendix C).

Swamp Fox Trail

Location:	20 miles north of Charleston in the Francis Marion National Forest.
Distance	13.3 miles one way.
Tread:	Wide singletrack with 6 miles on old railroad logging tram and 1.2 miles on gravel road.
Aerobic level:	Easy.
Technical difficulty:	1+; you might have to walk the tricky boardwalk sections.
Land status:	Francis Marion National Forest.
Maps:	USGS Awendaw, Ocean Bay, Huger; maps are available from Palmetto Trails and the Forest Service.
Access:	Follow U.S. Highway 17 north out of Charleston to Steed Creek Road (State Route 133) in Awendaw. The parking lot at the eastern trailhead is just past Steed Creek Road on the left. To reach the western trailhead, turn left onto Steed Creek Road and travel 7.4 miles. Park on the right on the gravel Dog Swamp Road. Hiker signs mark the trailhead, which is 0.2 mile further on the left.

Highlights

The Swamp Fox Trail, part of South Carolina's rail-trail system, follows old railroad logging trams for much of its length. You will need some patience to deal with the jolting of one bumpy stretch caused by crossties just below the trail's surface.

The trail travels deep into the Lowcountry's swampland. Enjoy marshy bogs thick with evergreens and drier ridges lined with open stands of pine. You can ride fast on this flat, wide singletrack with little concern of meeting any technical difficulties.

Local Scout troops built the original Swamp Fox Trail in the mid 1960s, and they continue to maintain the trail. Their handiwork includes mile markers, wooden bridges, and an elaborate boardwalk section. This trail is the first part of the 42-mile Swamp Fox Passage of the Palmetto Trail.

Swamp Fox Trail

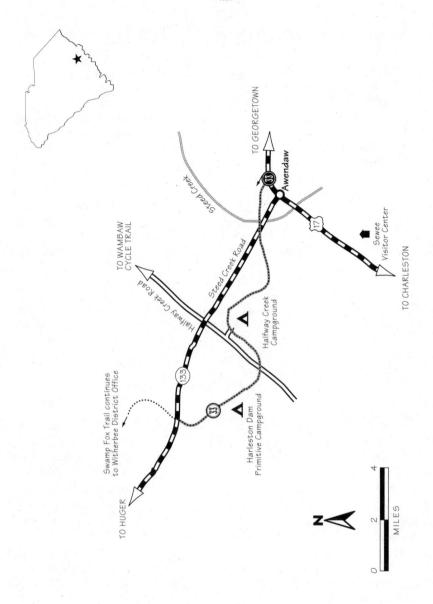

TO GEORGETOWN

Awendaw

Steed Creek

Sewee
Visitor Center

TO CHARLESTON

17

Steed Creek Road

Halfway Creek Road

TO WAMBAW
CYCLE TRAIL

Halfway Creek
Campground

133

Harleston Dam
Primitive Campground

Swamp Fox Trail continues
to Witherbee District Office

TO HUGER

N

MILES

0   2   4

Ben Jones gets ready to do a balancing act on the Swamp Fox Trail. JIM SCHMID PHOTO

THE RIDE

0.0 Go past an information board to begin the ride.
0.6 Cross a gravel road.
0.9 Cross the blackwater of Steed Creek on a wood and steel bridge.
1.7 Cross the paved Steed Creek Road.
2.8 Cross a gravel road.
3.3 Cross another gravel road.
3.7 Turn left onto a gravel road and ride 0.6 mile.
4.3 Turn left onto singletrack.
6.2 Ride through Halfway Creek Campground. Primitive camping and a hand pump for drinking water.
9.2 Cross the paved Halfway Creek Road.
9.8 Pass the Harleston Dam Primitive Campground.
10.6 Begin an elaborate boardwalk section through a marshy area.
10.8 A notice warns of nearby private property and hunting practices.
11.1 Cross a gravel road.
11.9 Cross another gravel road.
13.3 Reach the paved Steed Creek Road.

South Tibwin Loop

Location:	35 miles north of Charleston in the Francis Marion National Forest.
Distance	2.7-mile loop.
Tread:	Grassy roadbed.
Aerobic level:	Easy.
Technical difficulty:	1; sometimes the loop has sections of tall grass.
Land status:	Francis Marion National Forest.
Maps:	USGS Awendaw; a map is available at the Sewee Visitor Center.
Access:	From the flashing light in McClellanville, travel south on U.S. Highway 17. After about 3 miles, look for a paved road on the left with a gate. The parking lot and information board are just inside the gate.

HIGHLIGHTS

South Tibwin is a 600-acre tract of managed wetlands used primarily for wildlife viewing. Mountain bike access is allowed only on the designated

South Carolina's trails offer many unique challenges.

South Tibwin Loop

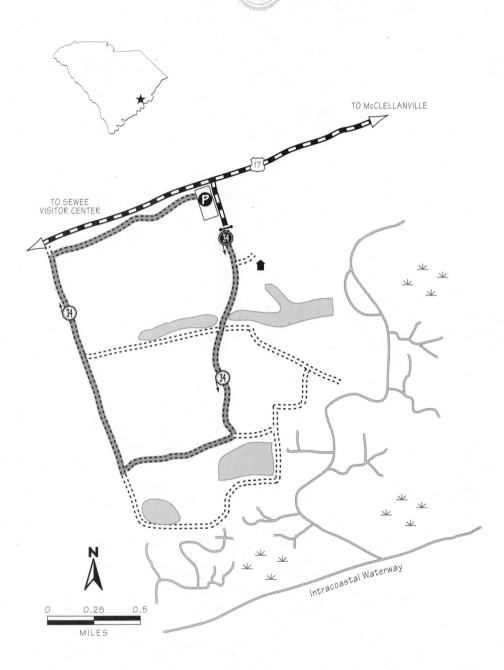

TO McCLELLANVILLE

17

TO SEWEE
VISITOR CENTER

P

34

34

34

Intracoastal Waterway

N

0   0.25   0.5
MILES

loop described here. In this part of Francis Marion National Forest you will experience hardwood bottoms, pine uplands, and tidal marshes. The Intracoastal Waterway borders the area to the south.

Wildlife blinds on the freshwater ponds allow you to see egrets, hawks, and ducks and if you're lucky, maybe a river otter or bald eagle. Be aware that alligators also frequent these impoundments.

Note: The area is closed periodically for special hunts. Also, call ahead to be sure the roadbed has been mowed recently.

THE RIDE

0.0 Ride around a closed (second) gate and head down a grassy road.
0.2 When you reach a house on your left, take a right.
0.6 At the first crossroads, continue straight
1.0 At a T intersection, turn right.
1.4 At the next T intersection, turn right again.
1.8 A road comes in on the right. Continue straight.
2.1 Turn right before U.S. Highway 17.
2.7 Return to the parking lot.

Charleston Department of Parks

The West Ashley Greenway came about when Charleston's Commission of Public Works obtained an abandoned railroad right-of-way from the Seaboard Coast Line in the mid 1980s. The City Parks Department agreed to maintain the surface as a greenway in exchange for use of the land as a park while the commission continues to use the subsurface for a utility corridor.

The parks department plans to continue improvements on the greenway's surface and possibly extend the path. You may ride West Ashley Greenway between dawn and dusk. For more information, contact the Charleston Department of Parks or the Bicycle Shoppe (see appendices A and B).

West Ashley Greenway

Location:	West of historic downtown Charleston across the Ashley River.
Distance	21 miles out and back.
Tread:	Wide, hard-packed dirt singletrack.
Aerobic level:	Easy.
Technical difficulty:	1.
Land status:	Charleston Commission of Public Works.
Maps:	USGS Charleston, Johns Island.
Access:	From downtown Charleston, head south on U.S. Highway 17 across the Ashley River. About 0.5 mile after the bridge, turn left on South Carolina 171 (Folly Road). At the second light, turn right into South Windermere Shopping Center. Park and pick up the trail behind the strip mall on the right.

HIGHLIGHTS

West Ashley Greenway parallels U.S. Highway 17 from South Windermere Shopping Center to Main Road, a few hundred yards short of the drawbridge over to Johns Island. This linear, grassy trail, once lined with rails and crossties, travels past neighborhoods, woodlands, and marshes. You will also ride through the middle of the Clemson Experimental Station, an extension office of the state's agriculture school.

West Ashley Greenway

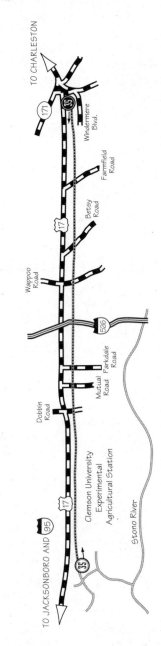

THE RIDE

0.0 Pick up the greenway behind the strip mall and head south.

3.8 The trailhead on your left accesses 2.5 miles of singletrack maintained by local riders.

5.8 Pass behind Clemson University's Agriculture Experimental Station.

9.8 A great fishing bridge.

10.5 Turn around and ride the greenway back to the shopping center.

Donnelley Wildlife Management Area

The 8,048-acre Donnelley Wildlife Management Area is situated at the headwaters of the Cheeha River, which flows into the Combahee River, one of the three rivers that make up the ACE (Ashepoo, Combahee, and Edisto) Basin. At Donnelley you will encounter the habitats that ACE Basin has to offer—managed wetlands, historic rice fields, forest uplands, and agricultural land.

The wildlife area was named to honor the late Gaylord Donnelley and his wife for their contributions to the ACE Basin project. The Donnelleys and other landowners, along with several organizations, cooperate through the ACE Basin Task Force to protect the landscape from development. A majority of the conservation project involves protective easements made up of over 25 old plantations along the Ashepoo, Combahee, and Edisto rivers.

Before riding at Donnelley, you must register at the information board in the office parking lot. Ask questions and get a map from the wildlife office, which is 0.5 mile farther on the main gravel road. You can ride every day but Sunday.

The Backwater Trail is open year-round, but the Boynton Trail is closed from November through January 21 to minimize disturbance to waterfowl. Scheduled hunts also close the area often during April and October. Closures are posted at the information board, but call ahead if you are driving any distance. For more information, contact the Donnelley Wildlife Management Area (see Appendix A).

Boynton Nature Trail

Location:	15 miles south of Walterboro in the Donnelley Wildlife Management Area.
Distance:	3-mile loop.
Tread:	Old roadbed and dike.
Aerobic level:	Easy.
Technical difficulty:	1; one slow section of soft, thick grass.
Land status:	South Carolina Department of Natural Resources.
Maps:	USGS Green Pond; a map of the trails in the management area is available at the wildlife office.
Access:	From Interstate 95 near Walterboro, take Exit 57 and follow the signs 2 miles to Walterboro; from there, take South Carolina 303 south for 15 miles to U.S. Highway 17. Turn left onto US 17 and take the first

Boynton Nature Trail • Backwater Trail

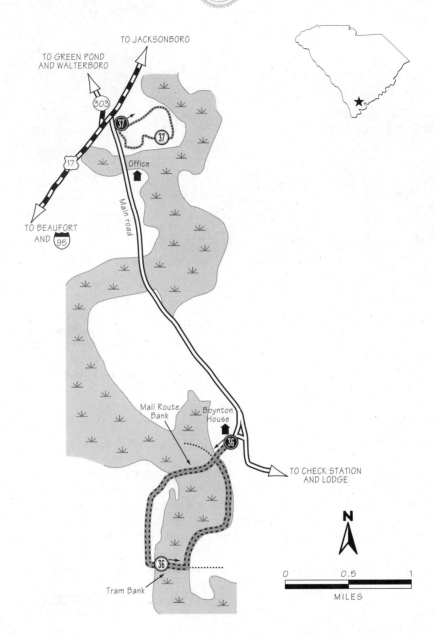

TO JACKSONBORO

TO GREEN POND
AND WALTERBORO

303

37

37

17

Office

Main road

TO BEAUFORT
AND 95

Mail Route
Bank

Boynton
House

36

TO CHECK STATION
AND LODGE

Tram Bank

36

N

0   0.5   1

MILES

The last leg of the Boynton Nature Trail.

right into Donnelley. Travel 0.5 mile on the main gravel road to the office on the left. After registering at the information board, continue another 2 miles to a nature trail sign. Turn right onto the grassy road and go a few hundred yards to a parking area across from an old white house.

HIGHLIGHTS

This ride begins at a turn-of-the-century farmhouse, a reminder of the Boynton family who raised free-range cattle here. An old road through second-growth pines and hardwoods takes you out to two (out of a dozen) impoundments that colonial planters cleared and constructed for rice cultivation. Water levels in the impoundments are now managed for wildlife; and vegetation such as widgeon grass and spike rush grow here to attract waterfowl. Hawks, ospreys, bald eagles, wood ducks, ibises, and wood storks use the wetlands.

First ride the dike out across the impoundment known as the Mail Route Bank, so named because the path was used to bring mail to the Boynton house. Then continue on the other side where regular burning creates open woodlands with giant loblolly, live oak, and hickory. Again, cross the open waters, this time on the Tram Bank, once a railroad tram that took logs across the wetlands to a major sawmill in Wiggins. Finish along a narrow canal, where it is not uncommon to spot an alligator.

Riding along the Tram Bank dike on the Boynton Nature Trail.

THE RIDE

0.0 Begin riding down the grassy road past the Boynton House and a nature trail sign.

0.4 Reach an impoundment, cross a small canal, and continue straight across the dike on the Mail Route Bank.

0.7 Veer left.

1.4 Emerge from the forest and ride across the impoundment on the Tram Bank.

1.7 Turn left and ride the grassy road along the edge of a small canal.

2.8 Trail junction. Turn right to return to your vehicle.

3.0 Reach the parking area at the Boynton House.

Backwater Trail

See Map
on Page 121

Location: 15 miles south of Walterboro in the Donnelley Wildlife Management Area.

Distance 1.5-mile loop.

Tread: Singletrack.

Aerobic level: Easy.

Technical difficulty: 1; newly cut with rough and uneven tread. This trail needs some riding time.

Land status: South Carolina Department of Natural Resources.

Maps: USGS Green Pond.

Access: Same as Ride 36. After registering at the information board, go back toward the entrance gate and park at the small lot on the right, 0.1 mile before U.S. Highway 17.

HIGHLIGHTS

This short ride, the newest trail at Donnelley, takes you through a thick pine forest. Because the trail was recently cut, the tread is somewhat rough and jarring. Watch for small stumps.

The trail's name comes from the location of the ride, bordered on two sides by freshwater reserves, called "backwater," which are part of an old rice plantation. Connect this loop to the Boynton Trail by riding the main gravel road, 2.4 miles of flat cruising. This gives you a total of 6.9 miles to explore at Donnelley.

THE RIDE

0.0 Pick up the trail just beyond the information board and enter a pine forest.

0.7 Begin curving around to the south. Hardwoods border the trail on the left.

1.5 Finish the loop back at the parking area.

Edisto Beach State Park

Edisto Island is a delightful place, isolated from the extensive resort development along the coast of South Carolina. You will find a few shops, several good seafood restaurants, and a string of modest rental cottages along the shore. The island is also home to the 1,255-acre Edisto Beach State Park.

The island lies between the North and South Edisto rivers, and between the Intracoastal Waterway and the Atlantic Ocean. Some of the tallest palmettos in the state border the beach inside the park, and an expansive salt marsh makes up much of the western part of the island.

Edisto is one of the oldest settlements in the state. The Edisto Indians lived here for thousands of years before they sold their land to the British in the late 1600s. The island is remembered for its sea island cotton, said to be the finest anywhere. Visit the Edisto Island Museum on South Carolina 174 to learn more about the island's history from the time of the early Indians to the 1920s, when the boll weevil destroyed all of the area's cotton.

The facilities at Edisto Beach State Park include oceanside campsites and cabins along the salt marsh. Also, enjoy a picnic area and the best beach access on the island, but expect crowds in the summer. A nominal parking fee is charged at the main entrance, but parking at the trailhead is free. For more information, contact Edisto Beach State Park (see Appendix A).

Note: The Spanish Mount Trail is officially an interpretive trail. The state park has not designated this trail for mountain bikers, although people are using it frequently for casual rides. Contact the state park before your visit for current information.

Bonus trail: In addition to the Spanish Mount Trail, you can ride on the beach at low tide north to Jeremy Inlet, 3 miles out and back.

Spanish Mount Trail

Location:	45 miles south of Charleston on Edisto Island.
Distance	3.2-mile loop.
Tread:	Singletrack.
Aerobic level:	Easy.
Technical difficulty:	1+; narrow trail, an occasional obstacle, and one sandy section (rated a 2) with drop-offs to the creek.
Land status:	Edisto Beach State Park.
Maps:	USGS Edisto Beach, Edisto Island; a trail map is available from the state park.

Spanish Mount Trail

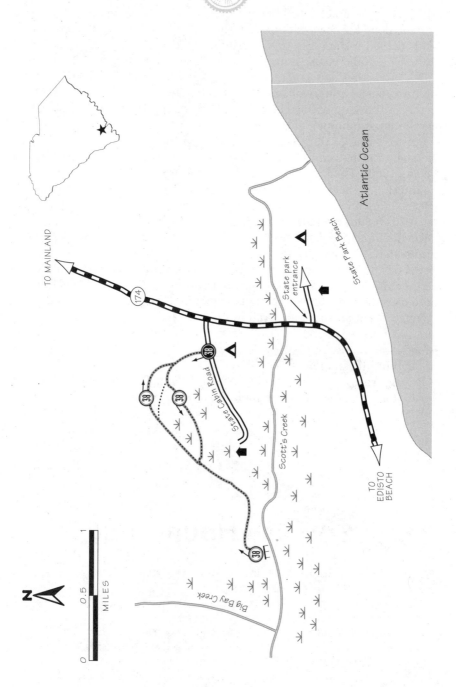

Atlantic Ocean

TO MAINLAND

174

State Park Beach

State park
entrance

Scott's Creek

State Cabin Road

38

38

38

38

TO
EDISTO
BEACH

Big Bay Creek

N

MILES

0   0.5   1

Access: From U.S. Highway 17, about halfway between
Walterboro and Charleston, travel south on South
Carolina 174 for 22 miles to Edisto Beach State Park.
After the first state park sign, turn right onto State Cabin
Road and go 0.2 mile to the parking lot on the right.

Highlights

This loop leads to cliffs overlooking a bend in Big Bay Creek where you can
visit an ancient Indian shell mound that dates back some 4,000 years. The
purpose of the Spanish Mount, which is similar to other middens along the
southeastern coast, is unknown, but theories range from social or ceremo-
nial significance to basically a trash heap.

Shellfish were important to the Native Americans, and recent studies on
this particular site confirm that the mound was actually a large circle, or
shell ring, which indicates a communal living area. Today, the shell mound
buckthorn grows in the high calcium soil generated from the shellfish. Please
don't walk on the mound.

On your way to the mound, you will traverse a beautiful salt marsh on a
long, wooden boardwalk and cling to the sandy open bank of Scott's Creek.
The flat, wooded singletrack winds through maritime forest where a heavy
canopy of live oaks, redcedars, loblollys, palmettos, and sassafrases provide
precious shade. Enjoy the junglelike feel of this environment with its Spanish moss and resurrection ferns.

The view from Spanish Mount overlooking a bend in Big Bay Creek.

A long, wooden boardwalk over a salt marsh in Edisto Beach State Park.

THE RIDE

0.0 Get on the singletrack just past the trail sign; and at the first junction, turn left on the unmarked trail.

0.4 At a trailside bench, take the left fork.

0.9 Ride the boardwalk across the salt marsh.

1.0 At the T intersection, go left again.

1.9 Reach the ancient shell mound and the banks of Big Bay Creek. Retrace your path to the T intersection.

2.7 Go straight through the T intersection to ride the other side of the small loop (continue straight at any other trail junctions).

3.2 Arrive back at the parking lot.

Hunting Island State Park

This 5,000-acre state park covers all of Hunting Island, a large barrier island east of Beaufort that includes salt marshes, freshwater wetlands, lush maritime and semitropical forests, and 4 miles of beach with some of the best shelling on the coast of South Carolina. The island gets its name from its historic use as a hunting ground. In 1938, the state obtained the island from Beaufort County to protect this valuable resource, and today Hunting Island is one of the state's most visited parks.

Hunting Island is home to a beautiful striped lighthouse, built in 1875 and active through 1933. Now listed on the National Register of Historic Places, this 132-foot structure on the north beach is open to the public. Climb its 181 steps for a spectacular view of the surrounding coastline and estuaries. Be sure to bring 50¢ for admission.

As for flora and fauna, slash pine and cabbage palmetto (the state tree), dominate the forest. A few resident alligators hang out at the visitor center and you might catch a glimpse of the island's dwarfed, white-tailed deer. Along the lagoon, look for brown pelicans, terns, herons, egrets, and shorebirds.

Facilities include oceanfront cabins and campsites, picnic areas, a fishing pier, a boardwalk, and a visitor center. A $3 fee is charged per vehicle from April through October. For more information, contact Hunting Island State Park (see Appendix A).

Hunting Island Loop

Location:	16 miles east of Beaufort in Hunting Island State Park.
Distance Tread:	7.8-mile loop.
Tread:	5.2 miles on singletrack, 2.4 miles on pavement, and 0.2 mile on the beach. (Optional beach miles replace most of the pavement at low tide.)
Aerobic level:	Easy; two sections of rolling hills.
Technical difficulty:	1 + ; soft sand, roots, and tight turns.
Land status:	Hunting Island State Park.
Maps:	USGS Fripp Inlet, St. Helena Sound; a map is available from the state park.

Hunting Island Loop

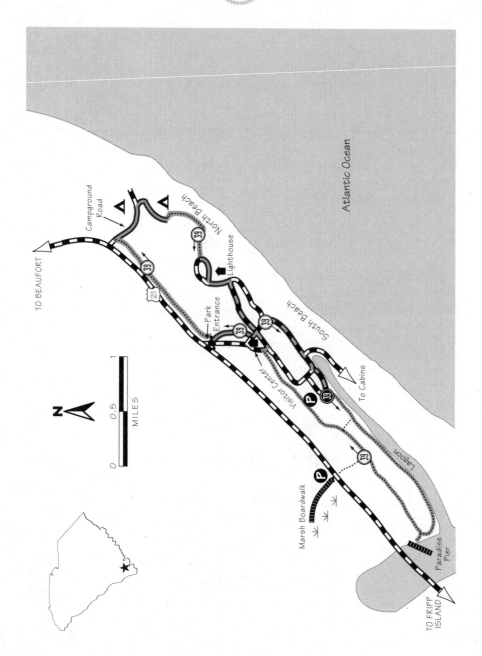

Access: From Beaufort, take U.S. Highway 21 to Hunting Island; the main entrance is about 1.5 miles on the left after a bridge. Drive past the turn to the visitor center and reach a four-way intersection in about 0.5 mile. Continue another 0.5 mile (past South Beach) to parking lot J. Veer left and go to the far end of the cul-de-sac to locate the trailhead on the left.

Highlights

Short sections of singletrack on Hunting Island can be connected to create a loop around the park, incorporating all the major highlights. Enjoy constant views of the water as you ride along an eroding bluff overlooking the lagoon. On the southern tip of the island, a spur trail leads to a 1,100-foot fishing pier, the longest free-standing pier on the East Coast; and Paradise Cafe, where you can stop for a bite to eat. Another spur trail accesses the park's Marsh Boardwalk Trail. The trail also passes the visitor center and the lighthouse. Finish with a swim in the ocean at South Beach.

This Lowcountry trail is surprisingly narrow and technical with soft sand, roots, and tight turns. Sections of gentle rolling hills add some interesting dips and berms.

Sandra Schmid in evening shadows at Hunting Island State Park. JIM SCHMID PHOTO

A lighthouse built in 1875 can be visited on the Hunting Island Loop.

THE RIDE

0.0   Follow a singletrack out along the lagoon.

0.4   At a trail junction, continue straight.

1.6   Follow the singletrack straight for a 1-mile out and back to the pier.

2.6   Return to the trail junction and turn left.

3.0   Follow the signs left, then right.

3.5   Arrive at the visitor center (straight across the boardwalk) and turn right on the pavement.

3.6   Turn left at a stop sign, then left again.

4.0   Immediately past a gate, locate the singletrack trail on the right.

4.5   Follow the big arrows right, then left.

5.2   Turn right onto the paved Campground Road.

5.4   Ride into the campground, past the camp store, and around to the right.

5.6   At campsite number 42, take the boardwalk out to the beach and go right.

5.8   Turn right into woods to ride the short singletrack to the lighthouse.

6.3   Begin riding on pavement.

6.4   Visit the lighthouse, then turn left and exit through parking lot E. (If the tide is low, turn right and go out to the ocean via a boardwalk. Ride on the hard-packed sand as far as South Beach, where you can leave the shore and return to your vehicle.)

6.6   Veer right.

6.7   Continue straight.

7.1   At an intersection, turn left and ride past South Beach.

7.6   Reach parking lot J and veer left.

7.8   Return to your vehicle at the trailhead.

Pinckney Island National Wildlife Refuge

Pinckney Island National Wildlife Refuge was established in 1975 and is managed by the U.S. Fish and Wildlife Service. For 200 years, Pinckney Island was owned by a prominent South Carolina family of lawyers and legislators. Major General Charles C. Pinckney, a signer of the United States Constitution, inherited the land in 1758 and ran a prosperous cotton plantation after he retired in 1801.

Today the area has reverted to its natural state and includes five islands and numerous small hammocks. Situated between Hilton Head Island and the mainland, this 4,053-acre wildlife refuge is 67 percent salt marshes and tidal creeks; and the high ground contains lowland forests, fallow fields, and freshwater ponds.

This haven hosts a large variety of birds—terns, oystercatchers, sandpipers, herons, snowy egrets, ibises, willets, gulls, and ducks. Pinckney is also home to several federally listed threatened or endangered animals, including the peregrine falcon, wood stork, and American alligator. Plant life consists of hardy species that can adjust to changing tides up to 10 feet. The refuge brochure lists six of the most common salt marsh plants and explains how to locate them.

Pinckney Island is open during daylight hours—the electric gate closes at sunset! There are no facilities at the refuge. Occasional closings include one special hunt and a few days of prescribed burning each year. For more information, contact the Pinckney Island National Wildlife Refuge office in Savannah, Georgia (see Appendix A).

Pinckney Island Ride

Location:	41 miles southeast of Ridgeland, just before the bridge over to Hilton Head Island.
Distance	6.8-mile loop and an optional 4.6 miles of out-and-back side trails.
Tread:	2.6 miles on grassy road and 4.2 miles on gravel road; side trails are all grass.
Aerobic level:	Easy.
Technical difficulty:	1; high grass on the eastern part of the loop can be frustrating.
Land status:	Pinckney Island National Wildlife Refuge.
Maps:	USGS Bluffton, Spring Island; a map is available through the refuge office in Savannah.

Pinckney Island Ride

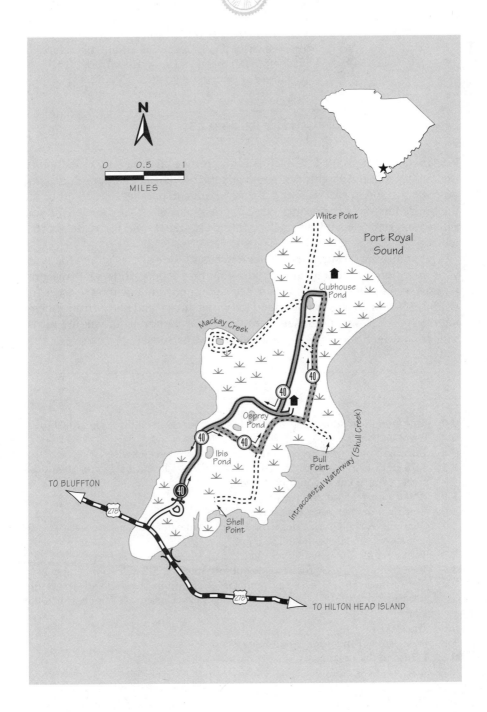

Access: Traveling south of Ridgeland on Interstate 95, take Exit 5 at Hardeeville and follow South Carolina 46 east to Bluffton. (SC 46 through Bluffton is a well-known speed trap. Keep it slow.) Then continue on to U.S. Highway 278. Travel east on US 278 for approximately 5 miles and turn left into the refuge just before the bridge to Hilton Head Island. The parking area is on the right after 0.5 mile.

HIGHLIGHTS

Pinckney, the largest of five islands in the refuge and the only one open to the public, is popular with runners, walkers, bicyclists, photographers, and bird watchers. A gravel road and a grassy path run parallel to each other for the entire length of the island. Several grassy roads off to your left, if you ride counterclockwise, lead back to the main gravel road to create shorter loops.

The nontechnical surface of Pinckney Island Ride allows you to focus all your attention on the outstanding Lowcountry scenery. Ride past freshwater ponds constructed to supply surface water and valuable food sources for wildlife. Nesting boxes are provided for wood ducks, and platforms for nesting ospreys. You will often see trees filled with hundreds of wading birds. This is a perfect ride for watching the sunrise or sunset.

THE RIDE

0.0 Ride around an orange gate and begin traveling north on the main gravel road.

0.7 Pass Ibis Pond.

0.8 Turn right on a grassy road to ride the loop counterclockwise.

1.5 Turn right to ride out to Shell Point (1.6 miles out and back; crosses a tidal creek) or turn left to continue the loop.

1.9 Reach a gravel road and turn right.

2.0 Veer right onto another grassy road.

2.1 Continue straight to ride out to Bull Point (1 mile out and back; to a grassy cul-de-sac) or turn left to finish the loop.

3.5 Turn left onto the main gravel road.

3.7 Turn right on a grassy road to ride out to White Point (2 miles out and back; to the northern tip of the island and views of Hilton Head Island across the Intracoastal Waterway) or continue straight past Clubhouse Pond to finish the loop.

5.0 Travel right.

5.3 Pass Osprey Pond, then Wood Stork Pond.

6.8 Return to the parking lot.

Appendix A: Resources

Anne Springs Close Greenway, P.O. Box 1209, Fort Mill, SC 29716; (803) 547-0234.

Baker Creek State Park, Route 1, Box 219, McCormick, SC 29835; (864) 443-2457.

Charleston Department of Parks, 823 Meeting Street, Charleston, SC 29403; (843) 724-7321.

Clemson Experimental Forest, Department of Forest Resources, Clemson University, Clemson, SC 29634-1011; (864) 656-3302.

Columbia Metropolitan Convention and Visitors Bureau; (800) 264-4884.

Croft State Park, 450 State Park Road, Spartanburg, SC 29302; (803) 585-2913.

Department of Natural Resources (South Carolina), P.O. Box 167, Rembert C. Dennis Building, Columbia, SC 29202; (803) 734-3888; website: www.DNR.State.SC.US.

Discover Upcountry Carolina Association; (800) 849-4766.

Donnelley Wildlife Management Area, Route 1, Box 25, Green Pond, SC 29446; (843) 844-8957.

Edisto Beach State Park, 8377 State Cabin Road, Edisto Island, SC 29438; (843) 869-2756.

Enoree Ranger District, Sumter National Forest, 3557 Whitmire Highway, Union, SC 29379; (864) 427-9858.

Greenville Parks and Recreation, P.O. Box 2207, Greenville, SC 29602; (864) 467-4350.

Harbison State Forest, P.O. Box 21707, Columbia, SC 29221; (803) 896-8890.

Hunting Island State Park, 2555 Sea Island Parkway, Hunting Island, SC 29920; (843) 838-2011.

International Mountain Bike Association (IMBA), P.O. Box 7578, Boulder, CO 80306; (303) 545-9011.

Long Cane Ranger District, Sumter National Forest, 810 Buncombe Street, Edgefield, SC 29824; (803) 637-5396.

Manchester State Forest, 6740 Headquarters Road, Wedgefield, SC 29168; (803) 494-8196.

McCormick Chamber of Commerce, P.O. Box 938, McCormick, SC 29635; (864) 465-2835.

Palmetto Cycling Coalition, Box 121, Summerville, SC 29484-0121; (864) 639-3607.

Palmetto Trails, 1314 Lincoln Street, Suite 213, Columbia, SC 29201-3154; (803) 771-0870.

Paris Mountain State Park, 2401 State Park Road, Greenville, SC 29609; (864) 244-5565.

Pinckney Island National Wildlife Refuge, U.S. Fish and Wildlife Service, Savannah Coastal Refuge Office, P.O. Box 8487, Savannah, GA 31412; (912) 652-4415.

Poinsett State Park, 6660 Poinsett Park Road, Wedgefield, SC 29168; (803) 494-8177.

Sand Hills State Forest, P.O. Box 128, Patrick, SC 29584; (843) 498-6478.

Santee Coastal Reserve, South Carolina Department of Natural Resources, P.O. Box 37, McClellanville, SC 29458; (843) 546-8665.

Santee-Cooper Counties Promotion Commission; (800) 227-8510.

Santee Cooper Land Division, 1 Riverwood Drive, Moncks Corner, SC 29461; (843) 761-8000.

Santee State Park, 251 State Park Road, Santee, SC 29142; (803) 854-2408.

Sesquicentennial State Park, 9564 Two Notch Road, Columbia, SC 29223; (803) 788-2706.

Sewee Visitor Center, 5821 U.S. Highway 17N, Awendaw, SC 29429; (843) 928-3368.

South Carolina Forestry Commission, P.O. Box 21707, Columbia, SC 29221; (803) 896-8892.

State Trails coordinators; www.sctrails.net.

Upstate Trail Riders Association, 123 Bennett Street, Greenville, SC 29601; (864) 235-8506.

Wambaw Ranger District, Francis Marion National Forest, P.O. Box 788, McClellanville, SC 29458; (843) 887-3257.

Wildwater, Ltd., P.O. Box 309, Long Creek, SC 29658; (800) 451-9972.

Witherbee Ranger District, Francis Marion National Forest, 2421 Witherbee Road, Cordesville, SC 29434; (843) 336-3248.

Appendix B: Bike Shops

Bicycle Shoppe, 280 Meeting Street, Charleston, SC 29401; (843) 722-8168.

Buddy's Schwinn Cycling and Fitness, 45 West Wesmark Boulevard, Sumter, SC 29150; (803) 773-8134.

College Cycles, 361 West Oakland Avenue, Rock Hill, SC 29730; (803) 329-0992.

Cycle Center, 2719 Broad Street, Columbia, SC 29210; (803) 798-7799.

Great Escape, 105 Franklin Avenue, Spartanburg, SC 29301; (864) 574-5273.

Sunshine Cycle, 106 North Clemson Avenue, Clemson, SC 29631; (864) 654-2429.

Appendix C: Bike Clubs

Augusta Freewheelers, 111 Dogwood Glen Road, North Augusta, SC 29860; (803) 278-6177.

Clemson Cycling Club, 110-A Old Central Road, Clemson, SC 29631; (864) 654-0688.

Greater Clemson Mountain Bikers Club, 13 Essex Drive, Clemson, SC 29631; (864) 654-6958.

Greenville Spinners, P.O. Box 2663, Greenville, SC 29602.

International Mountain Bike Association (IMBA), P.O. Box 7578, Boulder, CO 80306; (303) 545-9011.

Palmetto Cycling Coalition, Box 121, Summerville, SC 29484-0121; (864) 639-3607.

Sumter Chain Gang Cycling Club, 45 West Wesmark Boulevard, Sumter, SC 29150; (803) 773-8134.

Appendix D: A Short Index of Rides

Awesome Singletrack
1 Issaqueena Lake Trail
10 Tour de Dump
14 Lynches Woods Bike Trail
18 Turkey Creek Trail (South)
20 Steven's Creek Trail
21 Horn Creek Trail
24 Firebreak Trail
25 Harbison Loop
26 Sesqui Mountain Bike Trail
27 Sand Hills Mountain Bike Trail
28 Killer Three Loop

Technical Terrain
2 Dalton Road Ride
3 Figure Eight at Holly Springs
5 Quarry Trail
7 Johnstone Trail and Fox Trail
14 Lynches Woods Bike Trail
15 Parson's Mountain Motorcycle Trail (Right Loop)
16 Parson's Mountain Motorcycle Trail (Left Loop)

Rookie Rides
29 Lakeshore Trail
31 Bike/Hike Trail
35 West Ashley Greenway
38 Spanish Mount Trail
40 Pinckney Island Ride

Room to Explore
11 Springfield Loop
12 Enoree Off-Highway Vehicle Trail
13 Buncombe Trail
17 Long Cane Horse Trail
19 Turkey Creek Trail (North)

Race Routes
1 Issaqueena Lake Trail
8 Timmons Park Mountain Bike Trail
10 Tour de Dump
15 Parson's Mountain Motorcycle Trail (Right Loop)
26 Sesqui Mountain Bike Trail
28 Killer Three Loop

For Viewing Wildlife (Coastal)
31 Bike/Hike Trail
32 Marshland Nature Trail

34 South Tibwin Loop
36 Boynton Nature Trail
40 Pinckney Island Ride

Scenic Touring
1 Issaqueena Lake Trail
4 Fants Grove Lake Trail
21 Horn Creek Trail
23 Midlands Mountain Trail
29 Lakeshore Trail
31 Bike/Hike Trail
39 Hunting Island Loop
40 Pinckney Island Ride

Of Historic Interest
11 Springfield Loop
33 Swamp Fox Trail
35 West Ashley Greenway
38 Spanish Mount Trail
39 Hunting Island Loop
40 Pinckney Island Ride

Short Rides (under 3 miles)
6 Swine Farm Trail
8 Timmons Park Mountain Bike Trail
9 Firetower Trail
37 Backwater Trail

Multi-Day Rides
30 Lake Moultrie Passage
33 Swamp Fox Trail

Glossary of Mountain Biking Terms

ATB: All-terrain bicycle; a.k.a. mountain bike, sprocket rocket, fat tire flyer.

ATV: All-terrain vehicle; in this book ATV refers to motorbikes and three- and four-wheelers designed for off-road use.

Bail: Getting off the bike, usually in a hurry, and whether or not you meant to. Often a last resort.

Bunny hop: Leaping up, while riding, and lifting both wheels off the ground to jump over an obstacle (or for sheer joy).

Clamper cramps: That burning, cramping sensation experienced in the hands during extended braking.

Clean: To ride without touching a foot (or other body part) to the ground; to ride a tough section successfully.

Clipless: A type of pedal with a binding that accepts a special cleat on the soles of bike shoes. The cleat clicks in for more control and efficient pedaling and out for safe landings (in theory).

Contour: A line on a topographic map showing a continuous elevation level over uneven ground. Also used as a verb to indicate a fairly easy or moderate grade: "The trail contours around the canyon rim before the final grunt to the top."

Dab: To put a foot or hand down (or hold on to or lean on a tree or other support) while riding. If you have to dab, then you haven't ridden that piece of trail *clean*.

Downfall: Trees that have fallen across the trail.

Doubletrack: A trail, jeep road, ATV route, or other track with two distinct ribbons of *tread*, typically with grass growing in between. No matter which side you choose, the other rut always looks smoother.

Endo: Lifting the rear wheel off the ground and riding (or abruptly not riding) on the front wheel only. Also known, at various degrees of control and finality, as a nose wheelie, going over the handlebars, and a face plant.

Fall line: The angle and direction of a slope; the *line* you follow when gravity is in control and you aren't.

Graded: When a gravel road is scraped level to smooth out the washboards and potholes, it has been graded. In this book, a road is listed as graded only if it is regularly maintained. Not all such roads are graded every year, however.

Granny gear: The lowest (easiest) gear, a combination of the smallest of the three chainrings on the bottom bracket spindle (where the pedals and crank arms attach to the bike's frame) and the largest cog on the rear cluster. Shift down to your granny gear for serious climbing.

Hammer: To ride hard; derived from how it feels afterward: "I'm hammered."

Hammerhead: Someone who actually enjoys feeling *hammered.* A type-A personality who rides hard and fast all the time.

Kelly hump: An abrupt mound of dirt across the road or trail. These are common on old logging roads and skidder tracks, placed there to block vehicle access. At high speeds, they become launching pads for bikes and inadvertent astronauts.

Line: The route (or trajectory) between or over obstacles or through turns. *Tread* or trail refers to the ground you're riding on; the line is the path you choose within the tread (and exists mostly in the eye of the beholder).

Off-the-seat: Moving your butt behind the bike seat and over the rear tire; used for control on extremely steep descents. This position increases braking power, helps prevent *endos*, and reduces skidding.

Portage: To carry the bike, usually up a steep hill, across unrideable obstacles, or through a stream.

Quads: Thigh muscles (short for quadriceps) or maps in the USGS topographic series (short for quadrangles). Good quads of either kind can help get you out of trouble in the backcountry.

Ratcheting: Also known as backpedaling; pedaling backward to avoid hitting rocks or other obstacles with the pedals.

Sidehill: Where the trail crosses a slope. If the *tread* is narrow, keep your inside (uphill) pedal up to avoid hitting the ground. If the tread tilts downhill, you may have to use some body language to keep the bike plumb or vertical to avoid slipping out.

Singletrack: A trail, game run, or other track with only one ribbon of *tread.* But this is like defining an orgasm as a muscle cramp. Good singletrack is pure fun.

Spur: A side road or trail that splits off from the main route.

Surf: Riding through loose gravel or sand, when the wheels sway from side to side. Also *heavy surf:* frequent and difficult obstacles.

Suspension: A bike with front suspension has a shock-absorbing fork or stem. Rear suspension absorbs shock between the rear wheel and frame. A bike with both is said to be fully suspended.

Switchbacks: When a trail goes up a steep slope, it zigzags or switchbacks across the *fall line* to ease the gradient of the climb. Well-designed switchbacks make a turn with at least an 8-foot radius and remain fairly level within the turn itself. These are rare, however, and cyclists often struggle to ride through sharply angled, sloping switchbacks.

Track stand: Balancing on a bike in one place, without rolling forward appreciably. Cock the front wheel to one side and bring that pedal up to the one or two o'clock position. Now control your side-to-side balance by applying pressure on the pedals and brakes and changing the angle of the front wheel, as needed. It takes practice but really comes in handy at stoplights, on *switchbacks*, and when trying to free a foot before falling.

Tread: The riding surface, particularly regarding *singletrack*.

Water bar: A log, rock, or other barrier placed in the *tread* to divert water off the trail and prevent erosion. Peeled logs can be slippery and cause bad falls, especially when they angle sharply across the trail.

Whoop-dee-do: A series of *kelly humps* used to keep vehicles off trails. Watch your speed or do the dreaded top tube tango.

Index

Page numbers in *italic* type refer to photographs.
Page numbers in **bold** type refer to maps.

About the Author

Nicole Blouin is a professional freelance writer who specializes in outdoor sports. She spent ten years living and working on the Chattooga River in South Carolina, guiding raft and canoe trips. She spent two years as a columnist for *New York Outdoors,* and has published articles in *Currents* and *Canoe* magazines. She has a degree in physical education from Appalachian State University. *Mountain Biking South Carolina* is her third book.

get FALCONGUIDED

FALCONGUIDES® are available for where-to-go hiking, mountain biking, rock climbing, walking, scenic driving, fishing, rockhounding, paddling, birding, wildlife viewing, and camping. We also have FalconGuides on essential outdoor skills and subjects and field identification. The following titles are currently available, but this list grows every year. For a free catalog with a complete list of titles, call FALCON toll-free at 1-800-582-2665.

Mountain Biking Guides

Mountain Biking Arizona
Mountain Biking Colorado
Mountain Biking New Mexico
Mountain Biking New York
Mountain Biking Northern New England
Mountain Biking Southern New England
Mountain Biking Utah

Local Cycling Series

Fat Trax Bozeman
Fat Trax Colorado Springs
Mountain Biking Bend
Mountain Biking Boise
Mountain Biking Chequamegon
Mountain Biking Denver/Boulder
Mountain Biking Durango
Mountain Biking Helena
Mountain Biking Moab

■ *To order any of these books, check with your local bookseller or call FALCON® at **1-800-582-2665**.*

FALCON®

Visit us on the world wide web at:
www.falconguide.com